The IL
Divorce Survival Guide

Questions & Answers about your Rights
Before, During, and After Divorce

Fadi Baradihi, MBA, CFP™, ChFC, CLU, CDFA™
Nancy Kurn, CPA, JD, LLM, MBA, CDFA™

Edited by **Diana Shepherd,** Hon. BA

THE IDFA DIVORCE SURVIVAL GUIDE
Copyright © 2006 by IDFA Publishing, LLC

Address inquiries to:
The Institute for Divorce Financial Analysts™
24901 Northwestern Hwy , Suite 710
Southfield, MI 48075
website: www.InstituteDFA.com

Cover and interior design by Diana Shepherd

The Library of Congress has catalogued this edition as follows:

Baradihi, Fadi
    The IDFA Divorce Survival Guide / by Fadi Baradihi, Nancy Kurn, and Diana Shepherd
    / FIRST EDITION
       p. cm.
    ISBN: 0-9777404-0-4 (pbk.)
    1. Divorce—United States—Popular works
    1. Divorce—Law and legislation—United States
    I. Title.

Warning/Disclaimer
The questions and answers in this book may not apply to your unique situation. They do not take the place of a lawyer, accountant, therapist, etc. For professional advice, you *must* seek counsel from the appropriate professional. The authors and publisher shall have neither liability nor responsibility to any person with respect to loss or damage caused directly or indirectly by information contained in this publication.

CONTENTS

---

1.   What is a divorce?
2.   Do we both file for divorce?
3.   Can I file a petition for divorce in any state?
4.   Do we need a lawyer to get divorced?
5.   Can we both use the same lawyer?
6.   What are the grounds for filing for divorce?

[3]

CHAPTER 4 – PENSION AND RETIREMENT PLANS .. 38

CHAPTER 5 – SPOUSAL SUPPORT 43

[7]

FOREWORD

WHO is this book written for?

This book is written for anyone contemplating a divorce or in the process of a divorce.

WHAT can I expect to get out of this book?

This book will give you a general understanding of the different aspects of the divorce process.

WILL this book be all I need?

Reading this book will help you understand the divorce process. It will not, however, give you the knowledge to represent yourself. Unless your divorce is exceptionally straightforward – short marriage, no children, property, assets, or debts – you should not consider representing yourself. Some answers are in general terms because the law varies from state to state. You should get more specific advice from your lawyer, and, depending on your situation, other professionals.

WHEN should I read this book?

You should read this book when you sense problems with your marriage, and re-read relevant chapters during the divorce process. Learning about the divorce process will help you to understand your options if you are not able to save your marriage.

WHY was this book written?

This book was written because there is a need for a clear and concise explanation of the divorce process.

INTRODUCTION

WHEN A PERSON IS CONTEMPLATING DIVORCE, the fear of an uncertain future can take control of his or her decision-making ability. In most cases, once a divorce decree is signed, the divorce is final – and there's no opportunity to renegotiate an unfavorable deal. With time, most people will recover from the breakdown of their relationship; however, they will have to live with the financial decisions they made while under great emotional stress for the rest of their lives.

Some of the most common mistakes made in a divorce are due to a lack of understanding or analysis of an individual's short- and long-term lifestyle and saving needs, financial goals, and tax situation. It is not unusual for a divorced person not to know that he/she has access to retirement assets without early distribution penalties – or to find out, a few years after the divorce is final, that he/she can't afford to keep the house, put it up for sale, and then discover that he/she now has to foot the entire tax bill that should have been shared with his/her ex-spouse.

What's the answer? Education and the right professionals working for you. This book will answer many of the common questions that people contemplating divorce have about the process. It will not, however make you an expert. Do not gamble with your future: find the right professionals for your unique situation. A Certified Divorce Financial Analyst™ (CDFA™) can help you make better decisions. Using powerful software, they can value and divide property; evaluate whether or not you should keep the house; and help you to understand how retirement plans, pensions, spousal and child support guidelines, and tax laws apply to your situation. Most importantly, a CDFA™ will give you a clear view of your financial future and show you how to achieve the best possible outcome for you and your family.

Fadi Baradihi, MBA, CFP™, ChFC, CLU, CDFA™
President/CEO, IDFA™

Worksheet – My Priorities

If YOU DON'T REALLY KNOW WHAT YOUR PRIORITIES ARE, you won't know what to ask for – and what to fight for, if necessary – and what you can live without. Saying "I want it all!" is useful neither to you nor your lawyer. Use this worksheet to help you identify your priorities before entering into serious negotiations, and share this information with your lawyer. If you need more space, copy this worksheet onto separate pages of a legal or letter-sized pad; use the top half of each page to list your priorities, and the bottom half to list your spouse's. Add or delete items to suit your individual case.

Property division

My priorities are:	My spouse's priorities are:
a) _____	a) _____
b) _____	b) _____
c) _____	c) _____
d) _____	d) _____

Finances (spousal support, division of assets and debts)

My priorities are:	My spouse's priorities are:
a) _____	a) _____
b) _____	b) _____
c) _____	c) _____
d) _____	d) _____

Children (support, custody, visitation)

My priorities are:	My spouse's priorities are:
a) _____	a) _____
b) _____	b) _____
c) _____	c) _____
d) _____	d) _____

NOTE: if you and your spouse don't agree on custody, write down why you feel your custody arrangements are reasonable and in your children's best interest, and why your spouse's aren't.

1

GETTING STARTED

FOR MOST PEOPLE, the first time that they appear in front of a judge is for their divorce. This section will familiarize you with the legal process and introduce you to the different options that you need to consider.

1. *What is a divorce?*

A divorce is a civil action dissolving a marriage. It is also called Dissolution of Marriage.

2. *Do we both file for divorce?*

Only one spouse needs to file a petition for divorce. However, both spouses can file for a divorce as co-petitioners. The person who files the petition is called the "plaintiff" or the "petitioner." The spouse who is served the petition is called the "defendant" or the "respondent."

3. *Can I file a petition for divorce in any state?*

In most states, one of the parties is required to be a legal resident for a specified period of time before the judge will grant the divorce (See "Appendix A" for state-by-state residency requirements). As a result, if you are willing to wait, you can choose the state where your divorce will be granted. Your attorney can advise you about your options and the benefits of filing in different states.

4. *Do we need a lawyer to get divorced?*

No, but we recommend that you hire a lawyer to represent you. If you don't have a lawyer and you have agreed on a final property settlement with your spouse, then you should hire a lawyer to prepare the settlement agreement. There may be issues or ramifications that you haven't considered; a lawyer can make sure you completely understand the terms of your agreement, and can also help you to make the best deal.

5. *Can we both use the same lawyer?*

You should not use the same lawyer as your spouse. A lawyer is an advocate for his or her client; since there will almost certainly be areas in which your interests and those of your spouse diverge, one lawyer will not be able to represent both of you effectively. Your spouse's lawyer represents your spouse, *not* you, and "joint representation" may be detrimental to you.

6. *What are the grounds for filing for divorce?*

Most states have a "no-fault" divorce statute. To file a petition for no-fault divorce, you would state that your marriage is "irretrievably broken" or the parties have "irreconcilable differences" or are "incompatible." Generally, you must also show that you and your spouse have lived "separate and apart" for a certain period of time, which varies from state to state. Some states also offer "fault" grounds – such as infidelity, bigamy, or mental or physical cruelty. Ask your lawyer whether your choice of grounds could have any impact on the outcome of your case; if not, the separation period is the most straightforward and easiest to prove. (See "Appendix A" for state-by-state information about grounds for divorce.)

7. *What does "no fault" mean?*

"No fault" means that you are neither required nor permitted to show that the other party was "at fault" or did something wrong, such as committing adultery, or being mentally or physically abusive.

8. *What if my spouse won't agree to a divorce?*

The judge issues a judgment for divorce – *not* your spouse. Once you have filed the petition for divorce, your lawyer will serve a copy on your spouse. If your spouse does not file an answer within the statutory time limit (within 30 days, for example), then the judge will grant your divorce by default. If your spouse contests the divorce, then the two of you can testify at a hearing or hearings, and eventually the judge will issue a judgment of divorce.

9. *What should I do if my spouse is physically abusive?*

If you or your children are being abused, then you should seek help immediately! You owe it to yourself and your children to prevent any additional abuse.

10. *Where should I go for help?*

You should call your local mental health facility or crisis hotline for assistance; they can refer you to local resources. Do not hesitate to call the police if you are afraid of serious physical harm.

11. *How long does it take to get divorced?*

The time period varies according to state law. Some states have a "cooling-off period": this is the time period (commonly 90 days) you must wait before your divorce order becomes final.

12. *What happens after the petition is filed with the court?*

If you have reached a settlement with your spouse, then the paperwork is filed and the divorce is complete. This is called the "permanent order". If you cannot agree to a settlement, then a court date is set and a judge hears the case and issues a judgment of divorce.

13.   *How do you negotiate a settlement agreement?*

Generally, the spouses and each of their attorneys – or sometimes just the attorneys – meet to negotiate a settlement agreement. If the parties and their attorneys cannot reach an agreement on every issue, then they may go to court on the unresolved issues.

14.   *What should we do if we can't reach a settlement, but we don't want the court to make decisions for us?*

You can use your attorney to try to negotiate a settlement. Otherwise, you can use some type of alternative dispute resolution, such as arbitration, mediation, or collaboration.

15.   *What is the difference between arbitration and mediation?*

In arbitration, the parties hire a private judge to hear their case. Arbitration is usually quicker than litigation because you do not have to wait for a court date. In mediation, a trained mediator acts as a neutral third party and helps both spouses negotiate a settlement. The mediator does not give either party legal advice, but provides them with information to help them reach an agreement. Mediation works best when the parties are not extremely hostile toward each other and when they can reason with each other.

16.   *What is "collaborative law"?*

In this process, each spouse retains a collaborative lawyer to act as an advisor. The spouses negotiate directly with each other with their lawyers by their sides to offer advice and facilitate communication. Both parties and their attorneys agree at the outset that they will reach a settlement without going to court; if they cannot reach an agreement, both lawyers (and their law firms) must withdraw from representation. The fact that going to court is not an option tends to ensure that all the participants are truly committed to reaching a reasonable settlement.

17. *Does the judge decide our entire case if we can resolve everything except how to divide some of our property?*

No, the judge will only make a ruling on the unresolved issues. This can shorten a two-day trial to a one- or two-hour trial.

18. *What are "temporary orders"?*

Temporary orders are usually issued regarding child custody, child support, and spousal support. They cover the time period between the time that the divorce petition is filed and the time that the judgment of divorce is issued.

19. *What are "permanent orders"?*

Permanent orders are the final court orders ending the marriage.

20. *What happens if our divorce case goes to court?*

Each spouse will appear in court with his or her attorney. The attorneys will make opening and closing arguments. The attorneys will have the opportunity to question each witness by either direct examination or cross examination. Either side may also hire expert witnesses to testify.

21. *What is "direct examination"?*

Direct examination is when the attorney who calls the witness asks the witness questions.

22. *What is "cross examination"?*

Cross examination is when the opposing attorney asks the witness questions.

23. *What is an "uncontested case"?*

An uncontested case is a case where the defendant does not oppose the plaintiff's claim for the divorce or anything else that the plaintiff is asking for in the complaint.

24. *What is a "deposition"?*

A deposition is the taking of testimony in writing and under oath in preparation for trial. The attorneys for each side, the witness, and a court reporter are generally present at the deposition.

25. *What is "discovery"?*

Discovery is used to obtain information from the other side before trial. You can obtain documents or question witnesses through discovery. For example, you can get your spouse's checking account statements or retirement plan information through discovery.

26. *What if I don't agree with the judge's ruling?*

If you don't agree with the judge's ruling, you may be able to appeal the ruling. Your attorney can tell you if this is an option in your case.

27. *What should my attorney include in my divorce decree?*

Your attorney should include everything in your divorce decree that you need to completely protect your rights. It should address child custody, child and spousal support, asset division, and debt responsibility (see "Checklist: Final Divorce Decree" on page 87 for more information about this).

28. *After the divorce, can my ex-wife continue to use her married name or will she be able to take back her maiden name?*

Your ex-wife may ask the court for the right to resume using her maiden name. Even if she does not ask to take back her maiden name at the time of the divorce, she can file for resumption of her maiden name after the divorce is granted. In some states, it is much easier to change one's name during the divorce proceedings rather than afterwards.

29. *What is a "Certified Divorce Financial Analyst"?*

A Certified Divorce Financial Analyst™ (CDFA™) is trained to help analyze the financial outcome of a divorce. CDFAs are often Certified Financial Planners™, Certified Public Accountants, or attorneys with additional training on various financial issues of divorce, including: tax issues, retirement plans, division of property, and the financial effects of spousal support and child support. For the name of a CDFA™ in your area, call toll free 1-800-875-1760. You can also look for a CDFA™ on the Internet at www.InstituteDFA.com; click on "Find a Certified Divorce Financial Analyst".

Checklist – Getting Started

BEFORE YOU START NEGOTIATIONS with your spouse, you need to ask yourself some questions. Start with the worksheet entitled "My Priorities" (page 12) to give you the big picture, then narrow your focus to items such as:

❑ Who gets to stay in the home?

❑ Who will pay the mortgage (and other regular expenses such as gas, electricity, and home repairs) while you're apart?

❑ How will you share the money in your joint bank accounts?

❑ How will you share assets such as stocks and bonds? How about the pension(s)?

❑ Who keeps the family home/car/boat/washing machine, etc.? How will you split big-ticket items?

❑ What about the joint credit cards? You should cancel or freeze them ASAP. If you've never had credit in your own name, however, you should apply for your own credit card before the joint cards are canceled.

❑ How will you handle your current debts?

❑ Who will be responsible for the debts either of you incur while you're separated?

❑ Will you continue to file joint income-tax returns? Are there taxes due, or other problems pertaining to joint tax returns that will surface after the divorce that will have to be addressed in the division of property and liabilities?

❑ Will one of you be paying spousal support to the other? How much will it be? Will it be in the form of a lump-sum or periodic payments? When will the payments end? *Note: how you choose to pay spousal support can affect your tax status. Check with a lawyer before deciding how to handle this.*

❑ Will one of you be paying child support to the other? How much? When will the payments be made? When will they end (e.g., when the child turns 21, or leaves home, or completes college, etc.)?

❑ Will one or both of you be contributing to a college fund for your kids? How will the payments be made?

❑ How will you share responsibility for the care and raising of your children: joint, sole, or shared custody? When will the children be staying with each of you?

❑ Who will pay for legal fees? Will each of you be responsible for retaining and paying your own lawyer?

Checklist – Getting Organized

If DIVORCE IS AT YOUR DOORSTEP, you need to develop an organizational system that will work for you – and prevent you from drowning in a sea of paperwork. You will save time, money, and lower your stress levels if you can put your hands on a document the moment your lawyer or CDFA™ asks for it.

An accordion folder is a good way to keep everything in one place – and it's portable so your files can go with you to meetings. You will want to relabel some of the tabs so they're specific to your situation. For instance:

- ❑ Documents for my Lawyer
- ❑ Documents from my Lawyer
- ❑ Documents for my CDFA™
- ❑ Documents from my CDFA™
- ❑ Marital Property Inventory and/or Receipts
- ❑ Non-Marital Property Inventory and/or Receipts
- ❑ Household Inventory (use the Worksheet on page 35 to help with this)
- ❑ Household Bills and/or Receipts
- ❑ Bank Accounts (joint and separate)
- ❑ Credit Cards (joint and separate)
- ❑ Debts
- ❑ Monthly Expenses
- ❑ Income Statements
- ❑ Child or Spousal Support (paid or received)
- ❑ Insurance
- ❑ To-Do Lists

If you have never made a To-Do List, now's the time to start. There is simply too much to remember, and too much can fall through the cracks at this stressful time. There is computer software that can track tasks and appointments, or you can purchase a diary or appointment book that you will refer to every day. Make sure to put deadlines on everything: you don't want to keep your lawyer waiting for a document you promised last week because you forgot about it. To help get you started, see the "To-Do List" on page 100.

2

SEPARATION AGREEMENTS

YOU'VE PROBABLY HEARD someone say "I'm separated" many times in the past, but you've never really thought about what that means. Also known as a "settlement agreement," a separation agreement is a contract that spells out the terms of your divorce. This chapter explains what separation agreements can and can't do for you.

30.   *What is a "separation agreement"?*

A separation agreement is a contract between a husband and wife who have separated from each other. The agreement generally covers those issues that the parties have agreed on, such as the division of property and debts, custody, and child and spousal support. The separation agreement is frequently incorporated into the final divorce decree.

31.   *Who prepares a separation agreement?*

You should have your attorney prepare your separation agreement for you.

32.   *Can we divide our property in a separation agreement?*

Yes, you can address the division of property in your separation agreement, and it will be binding. The agreement can cover all types of property, including real and personal property and such items as bank accounts, stocks and bonds, retirement accounts and pensions, life insurance, and debts. However, in order to divide the property effectively, you may have to prepare or sign additional documents. For instance, you should change the names on bank accounts and change the titles on certain assets. A Qualified Domestic Relations Order (QDRO) may have to be prepared to change ownership of retirement accounts. Beneficiary designations need to be changed on retirement assets and insurance policies. In addition, any accounts that are set up with transfer on death beneficiaries should be changed.

33. *Is a separation agreement required in order to get a divorce?*

You are not required to have a separation agreement in order to obtain a divorce. However, if you can agree on child custody, child and spousal support and the division of your property and debts, then it is best to put this agreement in writing. This can speed up the entire process and your separation agreement can be incorporated into your final divorce decree.

34. *Does my spouse have to sign the separation agreement?*

Yes, both parties must sign the separation agreement. You cannot force your spouse to sign a separation agreement.

35. *How does a separation agreement help?*

In some states, if the parties enter into a separation agreement it may speed up the divorce process or make it less cumbersome.

36. *Can we specify who can claim our children as dependents in a separation agreement?*

Yes. For example, you can specify in your separation agreement that the non-custodial parent will claim the children; otherwise, the parent who has custody of the children for more than half of the year is entitled to claim them as dependents. The custodial parent can also waive the exemption, annually or for a period of years, by signing IRS Form 8332; in this case, the non-custodial parent must attach Form 8332 to his or her tax return to claim the children as dependents.

37. *If one spouse violates the terms of a separation agreement, can he or she be held in contempt of court?*

Unless the separation agreement has been made a part of the court order, it is not contempt of court to violate the agreement. Contempt of court applies when you fail to obey a court order without legal justification. If your spouse violates the separation agreement you may, however, be able to take your spouse to court for breach of contract.

38. *Can a separation agreement release me from liability for debts that I have incurred with my spouse?*

No. Your separation agreement is a contract between you and your spouse. Third parties, such as banks or finance companies, are not bound by a contract that you have made with your spouse. If your spouse agrees to pay a debt that both of you are liable for, but does not pay it, then you will still be legally responsible for that debt. You may take your ex-spouse to court for breach of contract to recover the amount that you paid.

39. *Will a separation agreement stop my spouse from hassling me?*

Probably not. Even though separation agreements usually have non-harassment clauses, no piece of paper will stop someone who is intent on hassling you. If physical violence is a problem, then a court order is more effective than a separation agreement. If the court order is violated, then the wrongdoer can be criminally prosecuted and punished.

40. *Can a judge modify the terms of our separation agreement regarding our children?*

Yes, the court can always modify the terms of your separation agreement regarding child support, custody, and visitation – particularly if it is in the best interest of your children. Unless it is proven otherwise, there is a presumption that the terms of your agreement are fair, reasonable, and in the best interest of your children.

41. *Is a judge bound by the terms of our separation agreement that do not pertain to our children?*

Generally speaking, yes: other terms can only be modified in very limited circumstances.

42. *Can we hire one attorney to prepare our separation agreement?*

We recommend strongly against this: one lawyer cannot be an advocate for both parties simultaneously since an agreement that is beneficial to one spouse will likely be detrimental to the other. Generally speaking, one spouse's attorney drafts the separation agreement and the other spouse's attorney checks to ensure his/her client's rights are protected.

Checklist –
Evaluating an Agreement

ALTHOUGH YOU WILL CERTAINLY ASK for your lawyer's advice, you are ultimately responsible for evaluating the draft agreements. Here are a few questions to ask yourself when considering a separation or divorce agreement:

Y   N

☐   ☐   **Is this agreement fair?** Apply this question to yourself – don't start trying to guess what your spouse might think about it at this point.

☐   ☐   **Is it in my best interests?** Is it in my children's best interests?

☐   ☐   **Can I afford this agreement** – now and in the foreseeable future?

☐   ☐   **Is there a clearly stated method to collect or enforce financial obligations?**

What did I want (see "My Priorities" worksheet, page 12) that I didn't get?

_____

☐   ☐   **Can I live without it?**
☐   ☐   **Is it worth additional time and money to renegotiate?**
What am I willing to give up in order to get the missing items?

_____

Am I rejecting this agreement because important provisions are missing or very unfavorable to me, or because I'm mad at my spouse and want to make him or her suffer? _____

Will I be better or worse off if I go to trial?

_____

Ask your attorney how a judge is likely to rule given your state's laws and guidelines.

☐   ☐   **Is the financial and emotional toll of *not* settling too high for me or my children to pay?**

3

PROPERTY

DIVIDING YOUR PROPERTY can be the most confusing and contentious aspect of your divorce. There are many factors that need to be considered, such as your short- and long-term financial needs. With proper analysis, decisions regarding asset division become easier. You must also keep in mind that you will have to live with this property settlement for the rest of your life, so seek professional advice before finalizing your agreement.

43. *What is "property"?*

Property is everything that you own, including your home, investments, retirement plans, antiques, and anything that you could sell or cash in for money.

44. *Is all property treated the same in a divorce?*

No, depending on your state, property is generally divided into two categories: marital property and separate property.

45. *What is "marital property"?*

Marital property is generally the increase in your net worth since the beginning of your marriage. Each state has a different definition of marital property.

46. *What is "separate property"?*

There are three kinds of separate property. Separate property is:
• Property brought to the marriage;

- Property inherited during the marriage;
- Gifts received during the marriage.

47.   *What is an example of separate property brought to the marriage?*

An example would be a mutual fund that you owned before you were married and you kept titled in your name. The value of the mutual fund at the time of marriage will remain separate property. However, in some states, any increase in value after marriage will be considered marital property.

48.   *What is an example of inherited property that was maintained as a separate asset during a marriage?*

Assume that, while you were married, you inherited a piece of property worth $50,000. If that property were bequeathed to you individually, it would be considered your separate property. However, in some states, any appreciation in value would be marital property.

49.   *What is an example of separate property that was received as a gift during the marriage?*

Assume that your mother gave you a stock that was titled solely in your name. This gift would be considered your separate property as long as it remained solely in your name.

50.   *Is bonus money that my husband received during our marriage, and put in a savings account in his name only, considered marital or separate property?*

Because the bonus was earned during the marriage, it would be considered marital property even though he put the money in a separate account.

51.   *Before I got married, I owned a mutual fund valued at $100,000 and I kept it solely in my name. It is now worth $150,000; how much of*

it is separate property and how much is marital property?

The original $100,000 is still considered separate property, because it was kept in a separate account. However, in many states the increase in value (i.e., $50,000) is considered marital property.

52. **What if money that I brought into the marriage was combined with my spouse's money and used to buy a house?**

Your house is considered marital property, and the money you used for the purchase – which was originally separate property – became marital property when you used it to buy the marital home.

53. **What if I add my spouse's name to the Deed of a house I brought into the marriage?**

You have essentially made a "presumptive gift" to the marriage. The house is now considered marital property.

54. **Before I got married, I owned a mutual fund. A couple of years ago, I sold it and put the proceeds into a money market account. Then last year, I invested the proceeds in a different mutual fund, still solely in my name. Is this mutual fund still my separate property?**

Yes. If you can trace the funds and they have always been kept solely in your name, then the mutual fund is your separate property.

55. **I took $50,000 from my mutual fund account and used it to buy a cabin with my spouse. After we sold the cabin, I took my $50,000 and added it back to my mutual fund account, which remains solely in my name. Is the $50,000 still my separate property?**

In some states, the $50,000 would still be considered separate property. In other states, the character of that money changed because you co-mingled it with a joint asset: the cabin.

56. *I gave my wife a 5-karat diamond engagement ring, which I consid-ered to be an investment for the family and marital property. She says that it was a gift to her and so it is her separate property. Who is right?*

This situation is not clear and the judge will have to decide.

57. *I inherited $30,000 and used it to buy a car, titled solely in my name, that we use as the family car. Is it still separate property?*

The judge could conclude that the car is separate property, because you inherited the money and kept the car in your name. However, the judge could also conclude that you made a gift to the family and consider the car marital property.

58. *How will the judge divide our property?*

In most states, there is a presumption that an even division of the marital property would be the most equitable way to divide your property. These states also give the judge the discretion to divide the property in any way that he or she deems equitable. The judge may consider factors such as contributions to the marriage (both finan-cial and taking care of the home and family), the tax consequences of the division, whether spousal support or child support is being paid, and the education, earning capacity, and health of each spouse (see "Appendix B" for more information).

59. *How does a 50/50 split of the assets work?*

If a 50/50 division is being sought, as you allocate assets to each spouse, the sum of each spouse's share should be one-half the val-ue of his or her total net worth. Each spouse should ask for assets that are going to meet his or her needs; for example, if the husband needs to finish his MBA, then a liquid investment such as a mutu-al fund or a stock account will make more sense than a retirement asset, especially if he is under age 59 1/2. However, remember that there may be taxes on distributions from the retirement account. So it would not be financially fair if one spouse ends up with all of the taxable retirement assets while the other spouse ends up with bank accounts that can be liquidated without any tax burden. If a 50/50 split is not feasible, then a property settlement note may be a good way to equalize both shares.

60.   *What is a "property settlement note"?*

A property settlement note is used to pay one spouse for assets he or she is relinquishing to the other spouse. This usually happens when one spouse wants to keep the family home, business, or pension plan and the other assets are not sufficient to make up for these assets. The other spouse is paid over time to make up for the shortage. The terms of the note can be negotiated, and an interest rate should be charged on the note. Because this is considered part of the property settlement, only the interest will be taxable to the recipient. Consult your tax professional regarding the deductibility of the interest. Here's an example: let's assume Mary wants to keep her business, which has been valued at $100,000. Her husband Bob is going to take their bank account, which is worth $20,000. To equalize their shares, Mary signs a property settlement note agreeing to pay Bob $40,000 over the next four years at 5% interest.

61.   *What are "career assets"?*

Career assets are benefits that someone receives or has as a result of his or her career. These include education, degrees, training, licenses, health insurance, disability insurance, life insurance, unemployment benefits, social security benefits, paid sick leave, vacation pay, retirement plans, pension plans, stock options, job experience, seniority, professional contacts, dues for membership in clubs, season tickets, and any other benefits from your employer.

62.   *Is a degree earned during the marriage a marital asset? If so, what is its value?*

In some states, a college degree earned during the marriage is a marital asset and judges are permitted to assign a value to the degree. In addition, in some states education levels are a factor in determining the amount of spousal support. Check with your attorney to determine the law in your state.

63. *What about a medical license or license to practice law earned during the marriage?*

In some states a professional license is also considered a marital asset. In any event, the increased earning power will be something the judge is likely to consider.

64. *How do you value household goods?*

Typically the fair market value of household goods is determined by using garage-sale prices.

65. *Who should get the house?*

Deciding who should get the house is an emotional as well as a financial decision. On one hand, there are emotional benefits – especially if children are involved – in staying in the house. On the other hand, the house is frequently the couple's biggest asset. Getting the house could very well mean getting nothing else. Having no spendable assets presents challenges as well. Most importantly, the house might be too expensive to maintain. Remember, unless changes are made, the same income that used to support one household now has to support two households. There are also times when it is more cost effective to keep the house: for example, if there is a small mortgage on the house and rent would be higher than all of the costs to maintain your current residence. All of these factors should be considered before deciding whether you should keep the house.

66. *How do we determine the value of our house?*

A real estate appraiser should be hired to appraise your house.

67. *Do we deduct the sales commission from the appraised value?*

Some judges allow you to reduce the value of your house by the sales commission. If your house is for sale, then judges are more likely to consider the sales commission.

68. *Can we deduct capital gain taxes from the value of the house?*

Most judges think it is too speculative to deduct the capital gain taxes from the value. However, if the house is for sale, then capital gain taxes should be deducted to calculate the value. The easiest and most equitable way to work this out is to actually sell the house and split the proceeds – then both parties share in the increase/decrease in value.

69. *Is life insurance an asset?*

Yes, if the insurance has cash value. Cash value is not the death benefit: cash value is the amount you get if you decide to cash in the policy. The death benefit is the amount that is paid at death. Cash value is found in "permanent" policies such as whole life or universal life insurance. Term life insurance does not have cash value.

70. *What if I suspect that my spouse is overspending?*

Tell your attorney immediately.

71. *What if I believe my spouse is hiding assets?*

Inform your attorney of your suspicions. Your attorney can bring a special legal action to discover the hidden assets.

72. *How do we handle our family business?*

It is imperative that you get a business valuation. Then you can decide if one of you will take the business or if it will be sold. It would be very difficult – impossible, if the divorce was acrimonious – for both of you to continue to run a business together after divorce.

73.   *Who should value the business?*

An appraiser or a CPA who specializes in business valuations should value the business. The valuation expert should be familiar with that type of business and your market area. You should not use the business' CPA, because it will be difficult for him/her to be impartial.

74.   *What should I do if I suspect that my spouse is hiding information regarding his business?*

You should start making copies of financial information regarding the business. This includes:
- Bank Statements
- Checkbooks and Canceled Checks
- Savings Account Information
- Income Tax Returns (both personal and business)
- Gift and Estate Tax Returns
- Financial Reports
- Applications for Loans
- Income Statements and Balance Sheets for the Business

Worksheet – Household Inventory

MAKE ONE PHOTOCOPY OF THE FOLLOWING PAGE for every room in your house. Then fill in the blanks as you decide who gets what: it will help you during your formal property division and let you know what you'll need to furnish your new home.

Room: _____ (e.g., Living Room, Master Bedroom, Kitchen, etc.)

Item	Description of item (Serial # if applicable)	Quantity	Purchased during marriage?	Current value (approx.)	Who is keeping it?		
					Him	Her	Dispute

Checklist – Charting Assets

A SSETS HAVE A WAY OF DISAPPEARING after divorce proceedings start. As soon as divorce becomes a possibility, start by listing what assets you think the two of you own. That list should include:

❑ **Cash.** Do you keep any at home or in a safety deposit box?

❑ **Checking account.** The list would include personal, joint, business, or trust accounts.

❑ **Savings or money-market accounts.** Don't forget accounts set up for a "special purpose" such as Christmas club or annual or semiannual expenses. These accounts are usually funded by payroll deductions and are set up to fund large and infrequent expenses such as the annual premium on your home or auto insurance, Christmas, and so on. These accounts are easy to forget.

❑ **Retirement accounts.** These include IRAs, defined contribution plans and pension plans (government and private). Don't forget any plans from previous employers that were left behind.

❑ **Non-retirement investment accounts.** These include mutual funds, brokerage accounts, annuities, cash-value of life insurance, certificates of deposit, and stocks or bonds held in certificate form.

❑ **Real estate.** This usually consists of the house and any other property owned by you and your spouse.

❑ **Employer-funded incentive programs.** These could include stock-option programs, country-club initiation fees, banked vacation, and sick days.

Once you have your completed list, start collecting statements for every item on it. Investment companies send statements monthly or quarterly, depending on the type of account, the level of trading activity, and the company's policy. Most employer-sponsored plans send out a year-end statement in the first quarter of the following year. So don't panic if a statement you're looking for doesn't show up at the end of the first month after you start the process. If you have a safety deposit box and you don't have a list of its contents, visit the bank and make a list.

Make a copy of the last mortgage closing paperwork. In order to qualify for a mortgage, you would have to disclose all of your assets, liabilities, and sources of income and the last five years' tax returns. Tax returns will show the sources and amount of income, especially if your spouse is self-employed. Income includes revenue from full- and part-time employment, investment return, and self-employment income. Add up all the income from different sources to come up with total income.

Worksheet – Charting Assets

MAKE ONE COPY OF THIS PAGE for each of the following assets you and/or your spouse owns: Bank Accounts (including investments and CDs); Retirement Accounts; Real Estate; Businesses; Vehicles; Patents, Copyrights, Royalties; Antiques, Art, Collections; Cash-Value Life Insurance; Licenses and Degrees (if applicable). Note whether Marital or Non-Marital funds were used to purchase the item under the "Source of Payment" category.

Type of Asset: _____

Description of asset	Date acquired	Titleholder	Cost	Source of payment	Value as of (date)

4

PENSION AND RETIREMENT PLANS

PENSION PLANS AND RETIREMENT ASSETS are frequently a couple's most valuable asset. The problem is that many people don't know how much their pensions are worth. This chapter explains how retirement plans work and how they are valued and divided.

75. *Are pension plans and retirement plans marital assets?*

Yes, to the extent they were earned during the marriage.

76. *How do I find out the value of our pension plans?*

There are several ways to find out the value of a pension plan:
- You can look at your statement from your employer. Statements are sent out in the first quarter of each calendar year. Some companies send out statements more frequently.
- You can ask your employer for the present value of your pension.
- You can hire a CPA, actuary, financial planner or CDFA™ to prepare a pension valuation.

77. *What is "vesting"?*

If an employee is vested it means that at least some of the retirement plan belongs to the employee and not the employer. This is the amount an employee is entitled to take when the employee leaves their employer. The portion that is vested comes from two sources:
- Employee contributions vest immediately. When an employee leaves his employer, he or she is entitled to 100% of his or her con-

tributions plus any earnings on those contributions.

- Employer contributions generally vest over a period of five to seven years. In the first couple of years an employee is generally 0% vested and after five to seven years an employee is 100% vested. Assume the employer has contributed $3,000 to the employee's account and it has grown by $500. Assume the employee is 10% vested and then decides to leave the company or is fired. The employee can take 10% of the $3,500 total value of the account (i.e., $350) in addition to any employee contributions.

78. *How does my pension plan work? My pension statement shows that I will receive $1,200 per month when I retire at age 65.*

Your pension is a defined benefit plan. Your employer contributes to your pension plan so that you receive a set amount at retirement time.

79. *I have a 401(k) account. Should I take out one-half of it and pay it to my spouse?*

No. You will be taxed on the distribution, and if you are under age 59 1/2, then you will probably have to pay a 10% penalty.

80. *What if I die soon after retirement?*

Before you retire you can decide if you want survivor benefits to be paid to your spouse or ex-spouse. If you elect survivor benefits, then your monthly payments will be less, because your employer will have to pay benefits for two life expectancies.

81. *What if I die before I am eligible to receive my pension?*

You need to review your plan documents. In some cases, the pension is forever lost and no one will be paid any part of your pension.

82.   *What is a "QDRO"?*

A QDRO (Qualified Domestic Relations Order) is a document that is required by federal law to divide employer-sponsored retirement plans in a divorce. The non-employee spouse may be awarded anywhere from zero to 100% of the retirement plan. Because the retirement assets are subject to income tax upon distribution, the retirement assets are frequently divided in half. A QDRO must contain the name and address of the alternate payee (the ex-spouse); the portion of benefits to be paid to the alternate payee (the ex-spouse); the period to which the QDRO applies; the plan to which the QDRO applies; and how the funds will be distributed.

83.   *How does the non-employee spouse get his or her portion of the retirement assets?*

It depends on whether it is a defined contribution plan or a defined benefit plan.

Example 1

If the retirement plan currently has cash value (this would be a defined contribution plan), it can be divided into two parts. One part is for the employee and the other part is for the non-employee. The non-employee can take cash. However, if the non-employee spouse does not keep the assets in some form of a retirement account, such as a 401(k) or IRA, then the account will be taxable. John has a 401(k) account with $320,000 in cash and securities. One half ($160,000) of his account is awarded to Mary. The other $160,000 will remain in John's 401(k) account. If Mary has her share moved directly into an IRA, then she will pay no tax on her share. She will pay tax when she starts receiving distributions.

Will Mary have to pay the 10% penalty because she took a distribution before age 59 1/2?

The non-employee spouse can take a distribution directly from the (defined contribution) retirement plan pursuant to a divorce and not pay the 10% penalty. If Mary were to have John's employer transfer her portion to her IRA or to a separate 401(k) account for her, and then she took a distribution, then she would pay the 10% penalty.

Will Mary have to pay taxes on her share?

Mary will have to pay taxes on her share if she does not have it directly transferred to an IRA or into her own 401(k) account. If she has it transferred into an IRA or her own 401(k) account, then she will not pay tax until she begins taking distributions.

Example 2

If the retirement plan is a defined benefit plan and has no cash value, then the non-employee will receive nothing at the time of the divorce, but will receive a percent of the monthly benefit when the employee retires. Example: Bill, age 56, is to receive $1,200 per month upon retirement at age 65. If there is a 50% split, then Bill will receive $600 per month at retirement and his ex-wife, Sara, will also receive $600 per month at that time.

If Bill continues working between the ages of 56 and 65 and his monthly benefit increases as a result, Sara will still receive $600 per month which is her half of the marital portion (the value at the time of divorce) and Bill will receive the remainder.

Checklist –
Pension and Retirement Plans

In MANY DIVORCES, the most valuable assets are future benefits such as pensions. Pensions and retirement accounts include:

❏ Individual Retirement Accounts (IRAs – no QDRO provisions)
❏ Defined contribution plans (requires a QDRO to divide)
❏ Defined benefit plans (requires a QDRO to divide)
❏ Retirement plans (government and private) such as PERS (Public Employee Retirement System), FERS (Federal Employee Retirement System), CSRS (Civil Service Retirement System), Military Pensions, and 457 plans
❏ Stock options (no QDRO provisions).

Don't forget any plans from previous employers that were left behind. These must all be determined and considered before starting to think about a settlement. In most cases, the marital portion of these benefits – in other words, the portion of the pension or other deferred benefits that have been acquired during the marriage – are subject to division as part of the divorce settlement. A good lawyer and CDFA™ will help you consider these benefits as part of the overall settlement plan, making sure your future needs will be met.

A couple of important notes about transferring IRAs:

❏ The division must be required by your separation or divorce agreement. If it's not part of the agreement, both parties will be subject to taxes and penalties.
❏ It must be rolled into another IRA to avoid taxes and penalties.

If you will be using a Qualified Domestic Relations Order (QDRO) to divide a retirement or benefit plan, your QDRO must contain the following information:

❏ The name and address of the alternate payee (the ex-spouse)
❏ The portion of benefits to be paid to the alternate payee (the ex-spouse)
❏ The period to which the QDRO applies
❏ The plan to which the QDRO applies
❏ How the funds will be distributed (to an IRA, or to an alternate payee).

If the funds will be distributed to an alternate payee, the funds will be taxable to the recipient unless he/she is a child or a dependent, in which case the parent pays the tax. The alternate payee would be your child or dependent if you are using the QDRO as security for child support; reasons to do this include the fact that your ex-spouse (the payor) is uninsurable, or doesn't want you to be named on his/her insurance. Ask your lawyer whether you should seek to secure your child support with a QDRO.

5

SPOUSAL SUPPORT

MOST STATES HAVE guidelines to calculate spousal support (also known as "alimony" or "maintenance"). However, judges have the discretion to determine first whether spousal support should be awarded, and if so, the amount of support and how long it should be paid. They may look at the amount calculated under the state's guidelines, but they will also look at need, ability to pay, length of marriage, standard of living, ages and health of both parties, number of minor children, educational level, and child support. Here's what you need to know about spousal support.

84. *What is the difference between spousal support, alimony, and maintenance?*

Spousal support, alimony, and maintenance mean the same thing. The terms spousal support and maintenance are becoming more widely used because of the no-fault divorce laws.

85. *Who pays the taxes on spousal support?*

Generally, the person who receives spousal support will pay ordinary income taxes on it and the person who pays spousal support deducts it from his or her income.

86. *How does a judge determine if I qualify to receive spousal support?*

In general, spousal support is based on state guidelines (see "Appendix C"). Of course, the guidelines vary from state to state, but here are some of the factors many courts are required to consider:

- The length of the marriage;
- The ability of the parties to work;
- The source and amount of property awarded to the parties;
- The age of the parties;
- The ability of the parties to pay spousal support;
- The present situation of the parties;
- The needs of the parties;
- The health of the parties;
- The prior standard of living of the parties and whether either is responsible for the support of others;
- General principles of equity;
- Fault.

87. *How do I determine my "reasonable needs"?*

You have to look at the whole picture. You cannot just look at the income potential – you also have to look at the assets. Here's an example: Mary and Bob have been married for 38 years. She is 59 years old and has never worked outside of her home. Mary appears to be a good candidate for spousal support. However, Mary received a two million dollar property settlement, therefore she is unlikely to receive spousal support.

88. *Do men ever receive spousal support?*

Yes. If a man has a reasonable need for maintenance and his ex-wife has the ability to pay, then he is a good candidate for spousal support.

89. *Is spousal support modifiable?*

Yes – if it is open-ended spousal support, which can be modified if your circumstances change. You can go to court and ask the judge to increase, decrease, or stop spousal support based on the changes in your circumstances.

90. *What is "non-modifiable spousal support"?*

Non-modifiable spousal support is paid in the exact amount specified and for the length of time specified, pursuant to an agreement by the parties or by court order. Once the terms are set, one party can never go back to court and ask the judge to increase, decrease, extend, or stop the spousal support.

91. *What happens if spousal support is to be paid for six years, but one spouse dies in year two?*

Spousal support must cease upon the death of the recipient; if it does not cease, then it will not be considered spousal support for tax purposes. Spousal support can be paid after the death of the payor, but most settlement agreements and divorce decrees state that it will stop upon the death of either spouse.

92. *What can the spousal support recipient do to protect against the payments ending with the payor's death or disability?*

The recipient can purchase life insurance or disability insurance with the payor as the insured party. If the payor dies or is disabled, then the recipient would receive the life insurance proceeds or the disability benefits. Sometimes the settlement agreement or the divorce decree requires the payor to purchase insurance for the benefit of the support recipient. If the recipient owns the policy, then the insurance premiums may qualify as spousal support for tax purposes.

93. *Will I still receive spousal support if I remarry?*

Open-ended spousal support will generally terminate when you remarry. Non-modifiable spousal support will be paid for the entire period it is ordered even if you remarry. Check with your attorney to be sure.

94. *Do I have to pay spousal support if my ex is living with a new romantic partner?*

Some settlement agreements and court orders provide that spousal support will stop if the recipient is living with someone. If it is not addressed in the settlement agreement, then you must pay spousal support as long as you are required to pay it. If spousal support is open-ended, then you may be able to ask the court to modify the order so it stops. Always check with your attorney before stopping payments.

95. *What is "permanent spousal support"?*

Permanent spousal support is paid during the recipient's life – unless you successfully petition the court to modify the order for permanent support.

96. *What effect does our prenuptial agreement have on our divorce?*

Your prenuptial agreement will generally take precedence over state law. The judge will look at state law and disregard your prenuptial agreement on such issues as child support, child custody, and visitation. Prenuptial agreements are not foolproof, however: the judge could set aside the agreement if he finds that it is invalid because it is unconscionable, or for any other reason that contracts are found to be invalid.

Worksheet – Spousal Support Log

MAKE COPIES OF THIS SPOUSAL SUPPORT LOG to help keep track of payments made, received, or missed; the first line is an example of how to fill it out. Put a check-mark in the last column ("Unpaid") if a payment is missed. In order to have a record, spousal support payments should be made by check rather than in cash.

Payment Period	Date	Check Number	Amount	Date Cashed	Unpaid
January 2007	01/01/07	057	$1,600	01/02/07	

Checklist – Spousal Support

If YOU WILL BE SEEKING SPOUSAL SUPPORT, you need to look for ways to minimize your own income while maximizing your spouse's, and to demonstrate that your sacrifices and contributions during the marriage allowed your spouse to get and hold a higher-paying job while keeping you in a low-to-no-income situation. Of course, you are *not* going to lie – but you *should* try to paint a picture of yourself as a responsible, self-sacrificing, terribly underfunded adult and your spouse as someone who can well afford – and deserves to pay – support.

In order to do this, collect the following information:

Your age: _____

The length of your marriage: _____

Will the children be living with you after the divorce?
❑ Full time   ❑ More than 50% of the time   ❑ 50% of the time
❑ Less than 50% of the time

Your state of health (both mental and physical): _____
_____
_____
_____
_____

Describe your job vs. your spouse's job, including salary and potential for advancement: _____
_____
_____
_____
_____

Outline your education, skills, and training. What would it take to qualify for a better job (what courses, length of study, apprenticeships, etc.): _____
_____
_____
_____
_____

Describe the contributions you made to your marriage (e.g., working to put your spouse through school, staying home with your children, entertaining your spouse's boss and/or clients to help advance his/her career, etc.):

_____

_____

_____

_____

_____

Describe the contributions you made to your marriage that reduced your current earning potential (e.g., quitting a job to stay home with your children, etc.). How much would you be earning today if you had stayed in the full-time workforce? _____

_____

_____

_____

_____

Did you sign a prenuptial agreement? If so, bring a copy of the agreement with you.

Describe any abuse in the marriage. Your lawyer will need to know if you were ever a victim or a perpetrator of abuse. _____

_____

_____

_____

_____

6

CHILD SUPPORT

CHILD SUPPORT CAN HAVE A BIG IMPACT on the financial survival of a family. Child support is meant to ensure that children can maintain the same standard of living after a divorce that they did while their parents were married. It is not intended to punish one parent for his/her misdeeds (real or imagined), or to allow one parent to avoid his/her responsibility to earn a living when the children are old enough to be left alone for periods of time.

If you will be paying or receiving child support, it is in your best interest to document the payments made/received. Even if you are making your payments to a state child-support-collection agency rather than directly to your co-parent, you should record every payment you make: state agencies make mistakes, and the punishment for failure to pay child support ranges from losing your driver's license to spending time in jail. Make copies of the "Child Support Log" at the end of this chapter to help keep track of payments made, received, or missed.

All 50 states have child support guidelines; although the guidelines vary from state to state, this chapter will explain some of the rules regarding child support and how it works.

97. *Is child support taxable?*

No, child support is neither taxable nor deductible.

98. *How does a judge determine the amount of child support?*

All states have Child Support Guidelines that are used to determine the minimum amount that must be paid (see "Appendix D"). The guidelines take into consideration the gross earnings of each parent, the expenses that each parent incurs for child-related expenses (from medication to private tutoring to summer camp) and how much time each parent spends with his or her children. Ask your attorney to explain how the guidelines work in your state.

99. *How long is child support paid?*

Child support generally ends upon the child's eighteenth birthday or upon completion of high school – whichever comes later. A couple may extend child support until a child has graduated from college or at a later age with their separation agreement or a court order by consent. If you have a disabled child, payment may be required for the duration of your child's life. Your attorney can review all of your state's rules with you.

100. *Can I reduce my child support payments when my child is staying with me?*

You should not reduce your child support payments unless your court order or separation agreement specifically provides for a reduction. Please check with your attorney regarding your child support payments.

101. *If my ex-spouse does not allow me to visit my children, then can I stop paying child support?*

No. Generally speaking, the courts consider child support and visitation two separate issues. In most states, you are not legally justified to withhold child support if your ex-spouse will not allow you to visit with your children. Likewise, if your ex-spouse is not paying child support, then you are not legally justified to stop your ex-spouse from seeing your children.

102. *Can my paycheck be garnisheed for child support payments?*

Many states permit wages to be garnisheed if child support is not being paid. You will have to go to court for any garnishment proceedings.

103. *My children seem to cost more as they get older; can I get an increase in child support?*

You can petition the court to increase child support. You will have to explain to the court that there has been a substantial change of circumstances requiring the additional support.

104. *Can child support also be reduced?*

Yes, you can request a reduction in child support due to a substantial change of circumstances.

105. *What is a "substantial change of circumstances"?*

A substantial change of circumstances includes a loss of a job, or a substantial increase or reduction in pay, or an increase or decrease in living expenses.

106. *Can child support include an annual increase for inflation?*

Yes, but it has to be spelled out in the divorce decree or settlement agreement.

Worksheet – Child Support Log

MAKE COPIES OF THIS CHILD SUPPORT LOG to help keep track of payments made, received, or missed; the first line is an example of how to fill it out. Put a check-mark in the last column ("Unpaid") if a payment is missed. In order to have a record, child support payments should be made by check rather than in cash.

Payment Period	Date	Check Number	Amount	Date Cashed	Unpaid
January 2007	01/01/07	057	$1,600	01/02/07	

7

CHILD CUSTODY

CUSTODY BATTLES are usually fraught with emotional landmines. If you and your spouse can't agree on custody and/or visitation (also known as "access" or "parenting time"), you should consider trying a few sessions with a mediator who has experience with these issues; if you can't resolve your differences, you will have to go to court and have a judge decide.

If you think you'll be going to court, you should start keeping detailed records of how your children divide their time – and whether you and/or your kids have any concerns about these arrangements. Unless your co-parent is truly dangerous – for instance, your ex is an abusive alcoholic/drug addict/criminal, raising genuine fears for their safety – you should recognize that children need *both* parents in their lives. So don't try to reduce your ex's time with the kids because you're angry with him/her. Instead, do whatever you can to foster a good relationship between your children and your co-parent: your children will be happier, and statistics show you're more likely to receive child support on-time and in-full if your ex spends meaningful time with his/her kids.

This chapter reviews various custody and visitation issues.

107. *Do mothers automatically get custody of their children when a separation occurs?*

No. This may be true in some jurisdictions, but most courts try to determine what will be in the best interest of the children before awarding custody to one parent rather than the other.

108.   *What factors do the courts consider in granting custody?*

The courts consider which parent was primarily responsible for caring for the children – including washing, feeding and clothing them, or helping them with homework – during the marriage and after any separation. They also look at how each parent disciplines the children, each parent's work schedule, and how each parent provides for their children's physical and emotional well being as well as their educational, religious, and social needs (see "Appendix E").

109.   *Can the custody of our children be changed?*

Custody is not permanent. However, the judge will generally only change custody if there is a substantial change in circumstances. The party petitioning for the change will have to prove that this change in circumstances has an adverse effect on the children.

110.   *Will my separation agreement prevent my ex-spouse from snatching our child and leaving the state or country?*

No. A separation agreement is only a contract – it is not a court order. If you violate a court order, you can be held in contempt of court; if you violate a separation agreement, it is merely breach of contract. If your ex takes your children to another state, you can file a court order in your home state and it will be enforced as if it were issued in the state where your ex is now living.

111.   *Will I get visitation rights if my spouse has custody of our children?*

The non-custodial parent will generally get reasonable visitation rights except in extraordinary situations: for instance, if the non-custodial parent has a history of abusing the child or if there is reason to believe that the non-custodial parent will not return the child to the custodial parent. In these cases, the judge may allow the non-custodial parent to have supervised visits with the children. If you and the other parent get along and can agree, then visitation can be very flexible and unstructured. If you do not get along with the other parent, then visitation may be very structured and rigid, with the times and days set out with great specificity.

112. *If one state awarded my spouse custody, can I file for custody in another state?*

No. Almost every state has passed the Uniform Child Custody Jurisdiction Act, which means that the court must inquire if child custody has been litigated in another state. If another court has decided custody, then the judge must refuse to rule on custody and the parents will be referred back to the original court.

113. *Will we have to wait until the divorce is final to resolve all custody issues?*

No. You can agree to your custody arrangement ahead of time, or you can get a temporary court order regarding child custody and visitation.

Checklist – Access Calendar

If YOU DON'T ALREADY HAVE ONE, buy a weekly or monthly calendar and hang it in an accessible spot to help you and your kids keep track of when they move between Mommy and Daddy's homes – or when they're visiting your ex if you have sole custody. If your children are young, you may find it helpful to use stickers to identify important events such as birthdays and holidays as well as when they'll be seeing their other parent. In fact, if you let them apply the stickers (with your help), your children may feel that they have a little more control over the process.

Buy stickers to represent:
- ❏ Time spent at Mom's house
- ❏ Time spent at Dad's house
- ❏ Time spent at Grandparents' house(s)
- ❏ Birthdays
- ❏ Holidays
- ❏ School field trips
- ❏ School tests
- ❏ Music lessons
- ❏ Little league games
- ❏ Girl or Boy Scouts
- ❏ Anything else important to your family.

This calendar can accommodate last-minute changes: you simply put a new sticker on top of the now-outdated one.

You will also want to buy a private daily planning notebook to record information for you (and your lawyer, if necessary) regarding how the custody and access arrangements are working out. Record the following information in this book:
- ❏ Missed or canceled visits
- ❏ Last-minute changes to the schedule
- ❏ Late pick-ups and drop-offs
- ❏ Any problems or concerns your kids have with the arrangements.

If your co-parent is consistently late, or cancels/skips/changes visitation frequently, you may have a good argument for changing the custody or access arrangements. When assessing your children's reactions to the current arrangements, bear in mind that your divorce, one or both parents moving, and a new schedule can create a great deal of stress for your kids. Give them time to adjust before pointing fingers and blaming your co-parent for their behavior. If they're really struggling, individual or family therapy or joining a group for children of divorce (such as those offered by Rainbows; visit www.rainbows.org for more information) can really help.

8

DEBT AND EXPENSES

PEOPLE GOING THROUGH A DIVORCE can be very nasty to their soon-to-be ex-spouses – and many try to use money to "punish" their exes. Perhaps you have heard about a spouse who put thousands of dollars in charges on a credit card after filing for divorce – and the other spouse was stuck paying the debt. You may have also heard about an ex-spouse filing for bankruptcy to avoid paying spousal and child support. The following information clarifies what happens in these and other situations.

114. *Who is responsible for debts that are incurred during the marriage?*

Generally, both of you will be responsible for marital debts.

115. *Who is responsible for debts that my spouse incurred after we filed for divorce?*

Generally, both of you will be responsible for these debts until the divorce is final.

116. *How can I protect myself if my spouse is incurring a significant amount of debt?*

You can request a special hearing to ask the judge for relief from your spouse's spending and to make him or her responsible for the debt. However, if your spouse fails to pay the debt, then your creditors will probably still hold you liable for the debt. In that case, you would have to try to get your spouse to reimburse you for any payments you made for debt that was his or her responsibility.

117. *If my spouse files for bankruptcy, how will this affect his or her obligation to pay a property settlement note? (See Question #60.)*

The property settlement note can be discharged in bankruptcy and your spouse would have no obligation to pay the note. However, if the note is secured by property (collateral), then you would have a right to the property. It may be a secondary right if another creditor has a prior security interest in the property. It is best to use property that appreciates as collateral.

118. *I have filed for bankruptcy. Will I have to continue paying child and spousal support?*

Yes, you will have to continue paying child and spousal support. These obligations cannot be discharged in bankruptcy.

Worksheet – Charting Expenses

THE FIRST STEP is to gather the necessary documentation that you need in order to be objective. This includes your check register and credit-card statements. As you list your expenses, make sure you don't "double dip." For example, if your cell phone bill is directly charged to your credit card, don't count your cell phone bill and the credit-card payment. An area that most people miss is cash withdrawals using ATM cards. You should be able to account for where that money was spent.

Make two copies of the expense chart (below), one labeled "Pre-Divorce" and one labeled "Post-Divorce." Start by creating your pre-divorce scenario, then go to the post-divorce chart and carry over each expense with an increase or decrease in its value. For example, if you now need to hire someone to do lawn care, this would be an increase. Food expenses, on the other hand, would decrease.

	Monthly Expenses	Annual Expenses
Home Expenses		
Rent/Mortgage	$_____	$_____
Homeowners/Association Fee	$_____	$_____
Home Equity Loan	$_____	$_____
Property Taxes	$_____	$_____
Telephone	$_____	$_____
Cellphone/Pager	$_____	$_____
Internet	$_____	$_____
Security System	$_____	$_____
Cable/Satellite	$_____	$_____
Electricity	$_____	$_____
Gas	$_____	$_____
Water/Garbage	$_____	$_____
Landscape Maintenance/Lawn	$_____	$_____
Snow Removal	$_____	$_____
Exterminator	$_____	$_____
General Home Repairs/Maintenance	$_____	$_____
Home Improvements/Upgrades	$_____	$_____
Housecleaning	$_____	$_____
Miscellaneous Household/Pool	$_____	$_____
Total Home Expenses	**$_____**	**$_____**
Food		
Groceries	$_____	$_____
Dining Out	$_____	$_____
Total Food Expenses	**$_____**	**$_____**

	Monthly Expenses	Annual Expenses
Clothing Expenses		
Clothing	$_____	$_____
Laundry/Dry Cleaning	$_____	$_____
Total Clothing Expenses	$_____	$_____
Entertainment/Recreation		
Entertainment (Excludes Dining Out)	$_____	$_____
Videos/CDs/DVDs	$_____	$_____
Hobbies	$_____	$_____
Movies and Theater	$_____	$_____
Vacations/Travel	$_____	$_____
Classes/Lessons	$_____	$_____
Total Entertainment/Recreation Expenses	$_____	$_____
Medical (portion not covered by insurance; excludes children)		
Physicians	$_____	$_____
Dental/Orthodontist	$_____	$_____
Optometry/Glasses/Contacts	$_____	$_____
Prescriptions	$_____	$_____
Total Medical Expenses	$_____	$_____
Insurance		
Life Insurance	$_____	$_____
Health	$_____	$_____
Disability	$_____	$_____
Long-Term Care	$_____	$_____
Home	$_____	$_____
Auto	$_____	$_____
Other (Umbrella, Boat, Cottage, etc.)	$_____	$_____
Total Insurance Expenses	$_____	$_____
Miscellaneous		
Postage	$_____	$_____
Gifts/Holiday Expenses	$_____	$_____
Vitamins/Non-Prescription Drugs	$_____	$_____
Toiletries	$_____	$_____
Beauty Salon/Hair/Nails	$_____	$_____
Pet Care/Vet	$_____	$_____
Books/Newspapers/Magazines	$_____	$_____
Donations	$_____	$_____
Memberships/Clubs	$_____	$_____
Miscellaneous	$_____	$_____
Credit Card	$_____	$_____
Total Miscellaneous Expenses	$_____	$_____

	Monthly Expenses	Annual Expenses
Transportation		
Auto Payment	$_____	$_____
Fuel	$_____	$_____
Repair/Maintenance	$_____	$_____
License	$_____	$_____
Public Transportation	$_____	$_____
Total Transportation Expenses	$_____	$_____
Other Payments		
Quarterly Taxes & Add'l Tax Payments	$_____	$_____
Spousal Support Payments	$_____	$_____
Child Support Payments	$_____	$_____
Eldercare Expenses	$_____	$_____
Professional Fees (Accounting, Financial Planning, Legal, etc.)	$_____	$_____
Service Fees (Banks, Investments, etc.)	$_____	$_____
Total Other Payments Expenses	$_____	$_____
Total Expenses (Excluding Children)	$_____	$_____
Child-Related Expenses		
Education/Tuition	$_____	$_____
School Lunches	$_____	$_____
Counselor	$_____	$_____
Sports/Camps/Lessons	$_____	$_____
Hobbies/Field Trips/School Activities	$_____	$_____
Toys/Games	$_____	$_____
Boy-Scout/Girl-Guide Dues	$_____	$_____
Clothing	$_____	$_____
Medical	$_____	$_____
Dental/Orthodontics*	$_____	$_____
Optometry/Glasses/Contacts*	$_____	$_____
Prescriptions*	$_____	$_____
Allowances	$_____	$_____
Miscellaneous/Haircuts	$_____	$_____
Total Child-Related Expenses	$_____	$_____

* Not Covered by Insurance

Total Expenses (Including Children) $_____ $_____

9

INSURANCE

MARRIED COUPLES USUALLY PURCHASE INSURANCE for peace of mind. If the breadwinner passes away or becomes disabled, his or her income can be replaced with insurance. When a couple divorces, the need for insurance may still exist. If spousal support or child support is being paid, the recipient may need to replace that income if the payor spouse dies or becomes disabled. Sometimes the insured will pay the premiums and they may be deductible as spousal support.

119. *Will my health insurance continue to cover our children and my ex-spouse?*

Your health insurance will not continue to cover your ex-spouse, unless he or she seeks COBRA benefits (explained below). However, your insurance will continue to cover your children, generally until they are 21 years old.

120. *What are "COBRA benefits"?*

COBRA (Consolidated Omnibus Budget Reconciliation Act of 1986) applies to companies that have at least 20 employees. COBRA permits your ex-spouse to get health insurance coverage from your company for three years after the divorce.

121. *Will I have to pay the COBRA premiums for my ex-spouse?*

Unless the court orders you to pay his or her premiums, your ex-spouse will have to pay the premiums. If your ex-spouse misses a payment, your employer can drop all coverage and is not required to reinstate the insurance.

122.   *What can I do if I am uninsurable and cannot get health insurance (other than COBRA)?*

Check with the insurance company that has your spouse's employer's policy to see if you can change the COBRA benefits to an individual insurance policy.

123.   *My spouse is changing her auto insurance to another company. Should I cancel the existing insurance on her vehicle to save money?*

DO NOT CANCEL ANY INSURANCE WHILE THERE IS STILL A NEED! The new insurance should be issued before you cancel the old insurance; you are better off doubling up on the payment than assuming the risk with no insurance.

124.   *My divorce decree required me to keep my ex-wife as beneficiary of my life insurance until our children are 21 years old. I have remarried and have a new family to support; can I change the policy to name my current wife as the beneficiary of the life insurance?*

You cannot change the beneficiary unless you obtain a new court order. If you want coverage for your new family, you will have to purchase additional insurance.

125.   *How can I find out how my divorce will affect my insurance coverage?*

You should read your insurance policy or ask your agent to explain how your divorce affects your coverage.

126. Should I continue to carry life insurance on my ex-spouse?

If you are receiving spousal or child support from your ex-spouse, then you may need to replace that support if he or she dies before those obligations end. You should also consider getting disability insurance on your ex-spouse, which would provide disability income if your ex-spouse requests a reduction in support due to a disability. If this is required by your settlement agreement or your divorce decree, then your ex-spouse will have to cooperate with you.

127. How can I get insurance on my ex-spouse?

Your ex-spouse would be required to pass a physical examination and cooperate in obtaining a policy or in transferring ownership of an existing policy to you. You will not be able to get insurance coverage on your ex-spouse without his or her cooperation.

Checklist – Insurance

HOW MANY INSURANCE POLICIES do you and your spouse have? Try to locate all of them, and fill out the following information for each policy:

Life Insurance
- ❑ Insurance Company and Policy Number: _____
- ❑ Agent's Contact Information: _____
- ❑ Type of Insurance: _____
- ❑ Expiration Date: _____   ❑ Premium: $_____
- ❑ Owner: _____
- ❑ Beneficiary: _____
- ❑ Death Benefit: _____
- ❑ Loans: _____
- ❑ Net cash value: _____

Health Insurance (including accident and major medical)
- ❑ Insurance Company and Policy Number: _____
- ❑ Agent's Contact Information: _____
- ❑ Type of Coverage: _____
- ❑ Expiration Date: _____   ❑ Premium: $_____
- ❑ Persons Insured: _____

Home or Renter's Insurance
- ❑ Insurance Company and Policy Number: _____
- ❑ Agent's Contact Information: _____
- ❑ Expiration Date: _____   ❑ Premium: $_____
- ❑ Named Insured: _____

Vehicle Insurance (car, truck, motorcycle, boat, snowmobile, etc.)
- ❑ Insurance Company and Policy Number: _____
- ❑ Agent's Contact Information: _____
- ❑ Vehicles Insured: _____
- ❑ Expiration Date: _____   ❑ Premium: $_____
- ❑ Named Insured, Owner, or Beneficiary: _____

Other Insurance
- ❑ Insurance Company and Policy Number: _____
- ❑ Agent's Contact Information: _____
- ❑ Type of Insurance: _____
- ❑ Expiration Date: _____   ❑ Premium: $_____
- ❑ Named Insured: _____

10

SOCIAL SECURITY

MANY RETIREES DEPEND ON SOCIAL SECURITY to supplement their retirement income. After you are divorced, you may still qualify for benefits based on your ex-spouse's income.

128. *I have never worked; will I qualify for Social Security after my divorce?*

If your spouse worked and you were married for ten years or more, then you are entitled to one-half of your spouse's Social Security benefits.

129. *I worked for only six years and contributed very little to Social Security; will my Social Security benefits be based on the amount that I contributed?*

You would be entitled to the greater of the benefit you paid in or one-half of your ex-spouse's Social Security benefits if your marriage lasted for ten years or more.

130. *If my ex-spouse remarries, will I still qualify for one-half of his Social Security benefits?*

As long as your marriage lasted at least ten years, you will still qualify for one-half of your ex-spouse's Social Security benefits.

131. *If my Social Security benefits are one-half of my ex-spouse's benefits, will that reduce my ex-spouse's Social Security benefits?*

Even though your benefits are based on the amount your ex-spouse paid for Social Security, your benefits will have no effect on your ex-spouse's benefits. For example, if your ex-spouse is entitled to receive $900 per month in Social Security at age 65, he or she will still receive $900 per month and you will receive $450 per month.

132. *Will I still be able to receive one-half of my ex-spouse's Social Security benefits if I remarry?*

No, your Social Security benefits will be based on your own contributions or your new spouse's Social Security benefits and not your former spouse's benefits. However, if you divorce your second spouse after ten years, then you will be entitled to Social Security benefits based on your own contributions, or your first or second spouse's contributions (whichever is greater).

133. *If my ex-spouse dies before age 65, will I still qualify for Social Security benefits based on my ex-spouse's Social Security contributions?*

If you were married to your ex-spouse for at least ten years and you have not remarried by age 60, then you will be entitled to full Social Security benefits based on his or her contributions – regardless of whether your ex-spouse remarried or remained single.

Checklist – Social Security

Do YOU QUALIFY TO RECEIVE SOCIAL SECURITY BENEFITS based on your ex-spouse's earnings? Here's a list of the criteria:

❏ You must have been married for at least 10 years

❏ You must be at least 62 years old (whether or not you have actually retired)

❏ If you're 62 years old but not actually retired, your divorce must have been finalized more than two years ago

❏ You must not have remarried (unless you married someone who is entitled to widow, parent, or childhood disability benefits)

❏ You must not be receiving primary benefits (as a result of your own earnings record) equal to or greater than half of those due to your ex-spouse

❏ You must not be receiving benefits from any other person's account – such as a previous ex-spouse to whom you were also married for at least 10 years. You can, however, choose which ex-spouse's benefits to claim (presumably, the one that will pay higher benefits).

If you meet these criteria, you are entitled to receive benefits whether or not your ex-spouse has remarried, or whether or not your ex-spouse is currently receiving benefits.

If your ex-spouse dies without having remarried, you might also be eligible to receive a widow's benefit. If you remarried at age 60 or over (or at age 50 if you're disabled), you may still be entitled to receive a widow's benefit from your deceased ex-spouse. You might also be eligible to receive a small death benefit to help cover burial expenses for your ex-spouse; ask your attorney about which survivor benefits you might be eligible to receive.

11

LAWYERS

One of the most important decisions you will make regarding your divorce is which lawyer to hire. As in any profession, there are good lawyers and bad lawyers. It is up to you to do your homework and to ask the right questions to find the best lawyer for your unique situation.

134. *How can I find a good lawyer?*

You will have to do some work to find a good family law attorney. Interview more than one attorney before deciding who to hire; after the initial interview, you should be able to answer these questions:
- Do I feel comfortable with this person?
- Does he or she listen to me when I talk?
- Is this lawyer interested in what my goals are, or only with his or her own goals?
- Do I respect his or her opinion?

Take some time to find an experienced attorney who is compatible with you – an attorney who understands and respects your thoughts and feelings about your divorce.

135. *Where should I look?*

- Ask friends or family members who are divorced for a recommendation.
- Ask your clergy or professionals such as your Certified Public Accountant (CPA), Certified Financial Planner (CFP™), or therapist for a referral.

- Observe local attorneys in court. You can contact the clerk's office to get hearing dates.
- Ask for a referral from the American Academy of Matrimonial Lawyers at 150 North Michigan Avenue, Suite 2040, Chicago, Illinois 60601, (312) 263-6477, www.aaml.org.
- You can also contact the American Bar Association at 321 North Clark Street, Chicago, IL 60610, (312) 988-5522, www.abanet.org.
- You can search Martindale Hubbell's on-line directory of attorneys by city, county or type of practice at www.Martindale.com.
- Contact your state bar association and ask if they have a referral service. You should look for members of the "Family Law Section" in your area. Some states have certified family law specialists; if your state has specialists, get the names of attorneys in your area.
- Call your local bar association; generally you can find the contact information in the White Pages or Yellow Pages of your local phone book. They may also have a lawyer referral service for family law attorneys. The referral service does not recommend attorneys based on their competence; generally, they are giving you the next three attorneys on their list.
- Of course, you can also look in the Yellow Pages of the phone book. Look for an attorney who specializes in family law.

136. What else should I consider?

- You should not use your spouse's attorney; he or she has a duty of loyalty to your spouse, not you.
- Don't share an attorney with your spouse – one attorney cannot fairly represent both of you.
- Don't use an attorney just because he or she quoted you the lowest price – cheaper isn't necessarily better.

137. Is it proper to "shop around" for an attorney?

Yes, it is proper to shop around for an attorney. You should be comfortable with the attorney that you choose to represent you. To determine if you are comfortable with an attorney, you will need to meet with him or her. Remember, the attorney you choose could affect the rest of your life.

138. *How much does a divorce cost?*

It depends on the situation; for example, if you have children or substantial assets, then the divorce would cost more than a divorce without children and without assets. If the relationship is very contentious and both spouses are fighting and cannot come to a settlement, then the divorce could be costly. It also depends on the attorney's hourly rate and if he or she is inclined to encourage a settlement.

139. *Is it appropriate to ask attorneys about their fees?*

Yes – in fact, this should probably be one of the first issues you discuss. The attorney should bring up the topic if you don't raise it. An attorney will generally give you an estimate of the time involved and his or her hourly billing rate. Keep in mind this is just an estimate: if any unexpected problems arise, then the estimate could be very different from the actual time involved.

140. *Is it true that most attorneys ask for their fee up front (a retainer)?*

Yes, it is prevalent in domestic relations cases. Sometimes couples reconcile and they don't want to pay for the work that the attorney has completed; by charging a retainer, the attorney can ensure that he or she gets paid.

141. *How can I prepare for my first meeting with my attorney?*

You will save money if you are organized and provide your attorney with concise and organized information. You should be prepared to discuss your marital problems. You should bring the following information to your first meeting:

- Family information, including the names and birth dates for yourself, your spouse, and your children, the date and county where you were married, and the amount of time you have lived in your county and state.
- An estimate of your finances, including income, expenses, assets, and liabilities.
- You should start gathering the information listed in "Charting Assets" (pp. 36 – 37) and "Charting Expenses" (pp. 60 – 62).

142. *What can I do if my spouse will not provide me with all of the information I need?*

Your attorney can obtain a subpoena and your spouse would be legally obligated to provide the information requested. As with any court proceeding, this would cost you additional money.

143. *Are there any questions that I should ask my attorney?*

You should ask your attorney the following questions:
- How do you bill?
- Can you estimate what your fees will be?
- Other than attorney fees, are there any costs that I will need to pay?
- How much do you think these costs will be?
- How many divorces did you work on last year?
- What percentage of your practice is divorce?
- What kind of trial experience have you had in divorce?
- Will an assistant do the work or are you going to work on it yourself?
- How will I be charged for your assistant's work?
- Who is the contact person in your office?
- What can I do to keep my fees down?
- How do temporary spousal support and child support work?

144. *Who pays my attorney fees: me or my spouse?*

Generally, you will pay your own attorney fees. You may get your spouse to pay your fees in the settlement agreement, but your attorney will want the retainer in advance.

145. *I can't afford to hire an attorney or expert witnesses. What should I do?*

Your divorce will affect your financial future. Therefore, it is imperative that you do everything possible to obtain funds to pay your legal fees and expert witness fees.

146. *Any final tips?*

- You should inform your attorney that you want him/her to be forthright with you and you do not want him/her to only provide you with information that he or she thinks you want to hear.
- Hire a new attorney if you are not comfortable with your current attorney.
- Don't call your attorney to vent; they will charge you for their time.

Checklist –
Initial Meeting with your Lawyer

BRING THE FOLLOWING INFORMATION to the initial meeting with your lawyer.

Personal data. Bring as much personal data about you, your spouse, and your children (if any) as you can gather. Write down:
• Your name (maiden name too, if applicable): _____
• Your spouse's name (maiden name too, if applicable): _____
• Your home address:_____
• Your home telephone number: _____
• Your age and place of birth: _____
• Your spouse's age and place of birth: _____
• Your Social Security Number: _____
• Your spouse's Social Security Number: _____
• Your state of health (both mental and physical): _____
• Your children's names and dates of birth: _____
_____
• If there are children from prior marriage, their names and custodial arrangements:
_____
• Length of time you have lived in this state: _____
• Your Green Card(s) and immigration papers (if applicable).

Facts about your marriage.
• When and where did you get married? _____
• Did you sign a prenuptial agreement? If so, bring a copy of the agreement with you.
• Have either of you been married before? Bring the details of your previous divorce(s) with you.
• What are your grounds for divorce (if applicable)? _____
• What is your date of separation? _____
• What are your objectives with regard to this divorce?
_____
• What are your spouse's objectives with regard to this divorce?
_____
• Name and address of the lawyer representing your spouse: _____
_____
• Was there any abuse in the marriage? _____

In order to represent you properly, your lawyer will need to know if you were ever a victim or a perpetrator of abuse. Knowing about the abuse also allows your lawyer to acquire orders of protection for you and your children.

Employment information.
• Your work address:_____
• Your work telephone number: _____
• Your spouse's work address:_____
• Your spouse's work telephone number: _____
• Your current employment and income: _____
• Your spouse's current employment and income: _____
• Your education/degree/training: _____
• Your spouse's education/degree/training: _____
• Your job history and income potential: _____
• Your spouse's job history and income potential: _____
• Your employee benefits: _____
• Your spouse's employee benefits: _____
• Your retirement or pension plans: _____
• Your spouse's retirement or pension plans: _____

Financial information.
• Joint assets of the parties
• Liabilities or debt of each party
• Life insurance of each party
• Separate or personal assets of each party
• Financial records including:
  ❏ Bank Statements
  ❏ Tax returns
  ❏ Applications for loans
  ❏ Investment statements
• Family business records including:
  ❏ What product or service does the business provide?
  ❏ Is it a sole proprietorship, C-Corporation, S-Corporation, LLC or partnership?
  ❏ List of shareholders, members or partners
  ❏ Percent of ownership in business
  ❏ Bank statements of business
  ❏ Tax returns of business
  ❏ Applications for loans
  ❏ Income and balance sheets
  ❏ Financial reports

12

TAX ISSUES

THIS IS SIMPLY AN OVERVIEW of tax issues that may arise due to your divorce. You should consult with your CPA regarding your particular situation and the current tax rules.

147. *How should I file my tax return?*

If you are still married, then you may file as "married filing jointly", "married filing separately", or "head of household". If you are divorced, then you may file as "single" or "head of household".

148. *My divorce became final on October 30. Am I divorced or married this tax year?*

You are considered divorced. You determine your marital status on the last day of the tax year, which is December 31 for most individuals. If you had your marriage annulled, it means that you were never married and you would file as either "single" or "head of household".

149. *Can I qualify as "head of household" if I am still married?*

You have to meet all of the following tests to qualify as "head of household":
- You did not file a joint tax return;
- You paid more than half the cost of maintaining your household for the year;
- Your spouse did not live in your home during the last six months of the year;

- Your home was your child's main home for more than half of the year and your child qualifies as your dependent unless you gave up the exemption to your spouse;
- You are a US citizen or resident alien during the entire year.

150. *Can each spouse file as "head of household"?*

Yes, if there are at least two children and both of you meet the tests above.

151. *Are there any advantages to filing as "head of household"?*

Your taxes will generally be lower if you file as "head of household" versus filing as "single" or "married filing separately".

152. *My husband earned all of our household income. He has prepared a joint return that he wants me to sign. What are the risks and benefits of filing a joint tax return?*

The risks can be substantial, because you are jointly and individually liable for any tax, interest, or penalties that are due on your joint tax return. If your husband had only W-2 income and you are sure he had no other income, and he has supporting documents for your itemized deductions, then the risk is limited, because he had taxes withheld. Overall he will probably pay significantly less tax if you agree to file a joint tax return. You could compromise and require that both of you go to a CPA to have your tax return prepared. If your spouse is a business owner, then the risks may be substantial. Even though the business income is his, you could end up paying taxes on his business income long after your marriage has ended. You should consult with your tax professional before agreeing to file a joint tax return.

153. *What are the risks and benefits of filing separate tax returns?*

If you file separate tax returns, your combined tax liability will generally be higher than your tax liability if you file a joint tax return. However, if you file separately, then you will not have any future responsibility for your spouse's taxes – which could be a significant benefit. You should definitely consider filing a separate tax return if your spouse has a business.

154. *How does a payment qualify as spousal support? How do you determine if a payment is spousal support or child support?*

The rules are very complex regarding the differences between spousal support and child support. Just because a payment is called "spousal support" or "child support" does not mean that the IRS will view it that way. For divorce decrees or settlement agreements executed after December 31, 1984, the following requirements must be met for a payment to qualify as spousal support:

- The payments must be in cash (this includes checks or money orders);
- The payments must be required by the decree or settlement agreement;
- The decree cannot state that the payments are not spousal support;
- The parties cannot be members of the same household when the payments are made;
- The payments cannot qualify as child support as defined by the Internal Revenue Code;
- The payments must cease upon the death of the recipient; and
- The spouses may not file a joint tax return.

155. *How can payments qualify as child support?*

If your decree or settlement agreement states that spousal support is to stop or decline upon the happening of an event related to your child, then the IRS says that the payments are really child support. For example, if your decree states that spousal support will drop by $1,000 per month when your child graduates from high school, then $1,000 per month is actually child support and it is neither deductible nor taxable, from the date it was first paid. It is also presumed that spousal support payments are really child support if the payments decline when a child hits certain ages, such as 18 or 21. You may be able to rebut this presumption, but you will likely require professional help to do so. There are additional rules that are far more complicated regarding child support; you should consult your CPA or CDFA™ before your settlement agreement is finalized.

156. *If I make the mortgage payments and my ex-wife continues living in the house after our divorce, could the payments be considered spousal support?*

Depending on the ownership of the property, you may be able to deduct the payments as spousal support.
- If the house is titled in your name, then the mortgage payments are not spousal support. Obviously, you could still deduct the interest and property taxes as itemized deductions.
- If the house is titled in your wife's name, then the payments are spousal support as long as they meet the other requirements.
- If the house is jointly owned as tenants in common, you would be able to treat half of your mortgage payment as spousal support (as long as the other requirements are met) and you would be able to deduct one-half of the interest and property taxes as an itemized deduction.

157. *If I pay the utilities for my ex-spouse, would these payments be considered spousal support?*

Regardless of who owns the house, if you meet all of the other requirements and you pay the utilities for your ex-spouse, the payments would qualify as spousal support.

158. *Who can deduct the medical expenses for our child?*

The parent who pays the expense can deduct the expense as an itemized deduction regardless of the custody arrangements or which parent claims the child as a dependent.

159. *Can both parents take the child care credit?*

No, the parent who has custody of the child for the greater portion of the year gets to take the child care credit for any child care expenses paid by the custodial parent, even if the custodial parent does not claim the child as a dependent.

160. *Can the custodial parent take the child care credit for expenses paid by the non-custodial parent?*

No, the custodial parent can only take the credit for expenses he or she pays. For example, Bob and Mary have a son, Alex, who lives with Mary and visits Bob on weekends. Bob pays Alex's child care provider directly. In this case, neither Bob nor Mary can claim the child care credit since she is the custodial parent, but he is paying for the child care.

161. *Can I deduct any of the legal costs I incurred to get divorced?*

You cannot deduct the legal fees or court costs for the divorce. However, you can deduct any fees, including legal fees, that were paid for tax advice related to the divorce or to help you get spousal support.

162. *Can I deduct any other costs related to the divorce?*

Yes, you may be able to deduct fees you paid to CPAs, CDFAs, appraisers, actuaries and financial planners for services to determine your correct tax or to help you get spousal support.

163. *How do I know what amount of my fees are tax deductible?*

You should ask your attorney to break down, in writing, the amount of his or her fee that was related to tax planning or spousal support. You can also add any fees associated with your property settlement to the cost basis of your property.

164. *How can I find out more about taxes?*

You can speak to your CPA or to a CDFA™; they can explain how the rules relate to your particular situation. You can also look on the Internet or purchase tax guides or obtain tax publications for free from the IRS. Here are some IRS tax publications that may be helpful:

Publication Name	Publication Number
Your Federal Income Tax	17
Divorced or Separated Individuals	504
Moving Expenses	521
Selling Your Home	523
Individual Retirement Arrangements	590

Checklist - Tax Issues

Filing Status
- *Single:* Generally, divorce or legal separation must be final by December 31.
- *Married Filing Separate:* Generally, this will be the costliest way to file.
- *Married Filing Joint:* Cannot be divorced on or before December 31.
- *Head of Household:* This is generally the most favorable way to file. You must provide a residence for more than half of the year for a qualifying child or dependent.

Support
Spousal support is taxable to the recipient and deductible by the payor. Child support, however, is not deductible by either parent. You can't disguise your child support as spousal support to get the more favorable tax treatment; if spousal support ends on or close to some milestone in your child's life – such as when a child turns 18, leaves school or home – it will be reclassified as child support.

Children
Claiming the child as a dependent
- This can be spelled out in the divorce decree.
- If not spelled out in the divorce decree, then the parent who has custody of the child for more than 50% of the year claims the child. In the year of the divorce or separation, this is measured during the period the parents are separated or divorced.
- By the consent of the parent that has the child for more than 50% of the year. You must attach a signed copy of Form 8332 (Release of Claim to Exemption for Child of Divorced or Separated Parents) to the tax return.

Medical expenses
- Generally, the parent that pays the medical expenses can take the deduction, regardless of which parent claims the child as a dependent.

Child Care Credit, Child Tax Credit, Hope and Lifetime Learning Credits
- The custodial parent can take the child care credit for the amounts he/she pays for child care for children under age 13. You can still qualify, even if your ex-spouse claims the child as a dependent. You cannot include the amounts paid by your ex-spouse.
- You have to claim the child as a dependent to take the Child Tax Credit.
- The parent who claims the child as a dependent qualifies for the learning credits. If the child is not claimed as a dependent, then the child qualifies for the credits.

Legal expenses
- Generally, only those expenses related to obtaining spousal support are deductible. If the expenses relate to a business and the tax effect of dividing the business and its assets, they may also be deductible.

Transfer of assets
Generally, there is no gain or loss on the transfer of property to a spouse or ex-spouse if it is incident to a divorce. There could be tax if business or rental property is transferred.

13

INDIVIDUAL RETIREMENT ACCOUNTS (IRAs)

THERE IS A LOT OF CONFUSION about how Individual Retirement Accounts (IRAs) are treated in divorce; this chapter will answer your basic questions about IRAs.

165. *Are our IRAs marital property?*

Yes. IRAs – just like your pensions, 401(k) plans and all other types of retirement assets and deferred compensation – can be marital property. If you or your spouse contributed to your IRAs during the marriage, then that part is marital property. Any part that existed prior to the marriage would be separate property. However, the earnings on the separate property may be marital property depending on your state law.

166. *How can my IRA be transferred to my spouse? Do I have to pay penalties or taxes on the transfer?*

If your spouse is getting 100% of a particular IRA account, then you can change the name on that IRA to your spouse's name. You can also have the trustee (the bank or investment company) transfer your spouse's share of the IRA to a new or existing IRA in your spouse's name. Another option is to have the trustee transfer your portion to a new IRA and then have them change the name on your original IRA to your spouse's name. Do not take a distribution out of your IRA to give it to your spouse. If you are under age 59 1/2, you will end up paying taxes and penalties on the distribution; your spouse, how-ever, will end up with tax-free cash.

167. *I understand that my spouse can take a distribution from my 401(k) plan and pay taxes, but no penalty on the distribution. Do the same rules apply to IRAs?*

No, only distributions that are made pursuant to a QDRO (Qualified Domestic Relations Order) qualify under these rules. QDROs are not used to divide IRAs. If your spouse is under age 59 1/2, then your spouse will be subject to the 10% penalty in addition to the tax-es on any distributions from IRAs.

168. *We have always contributed to a spousal IRA for my wife. Can she still contribute to an IRA?*

In the year your divorce is final, she will need earned income to contribute to an IRA. Spousal support qualifies as earned income, so she would be able to contribute to her IRA if you are paying spousal support.

169. *Will I be able to deduct the contribution to my wife's spousal IRA in the year our divorce is final?*

No, you cannot deduct the contribution you made to your ex-wife's IRA. However, she can take the deduction on her tax return.

Checklist — IRAs

❑ IRA contributions during the marriage are marital property.

❑ IRA contributions before the marriage are separate property. However, the growth may be marital property depending on state law.

❑ A QDRO (Qualified Domestic Relations Order) is not used to divide an IRA.

❑ Transfer of an IRA pursuant to the divorce decree is not a taxable transfer.

❑ Alimony is considered earned income for purposes of determining the IRA contribution deduction limit.

Checklist – Final Divorce Decree

U SE THIS LIST OF QUESTIONS to ensure that your divorce decree addresses those issues that are important to you.

The Divorce Process
❑ Who pays your legal fees?
❑ Will the person who is not complying with the divorce decree be responsible for the other party's legal fees and court costs to enforce the decree?
❑ Do you want interest to be charged if one spouse is not paying alimony or child support?

Property
❑ How are you dividing the property?
❑ How are you dividing the debt?
❑ Have QDROs been prepared to divide pensions and other retirement assets?
❑ Should there be collateral for the property settlement note?
❑ Are you charging interest on the property settlement note?
❑ What is the cost basis of your house and other assets?
❑ If you get the house and you need to sell it immediately, will you be responsible for the entire capital gains tax?

Spousal Support
❑ How much spousal support is being paid and for what time period?
❑ Can spousal support be awarded later?
❑ Will life insurance or disability insurance be used to cover the loss of spousal support due to the payor's death or disability?

Child Support
❑ How much child support is being paid and for what time period?
❑ Will child support change when visitation occurs?
❑ Will child support be paid when the children are in college?
❑ Who has custody of the children?
❑ What is the visitation schedule?
❑ Who pays for the children's expenses for school (transportation, books) and unusual expenses (lessons, camp, orthodontics)?
❑ Who gets the exemption for the children on income tax returns?

APPENDIX A

GROUNDS FOR DIVORCE AND RESIDENCY REQUIREMENTS

	No Fault Sole Ground	No Fault Added to Traditional	Incompatibility Formula	Living Separate and Apart	Judicial Separation	Durational Requirements
Alabama		X	X	2 years	X	6 months
Alaska	X	X	X	2 years	X	6 months
Arizona	X	X			X	90 days
Arkansas		X		18 months	X	60 days
California	X				X	6 months
Colorado	X				X	90 days
Connecticut		X		18 months	X	1 year
Delaware		X	X	6 months		6 months
D.C.	X			1 year	X	6 months
Florida	X					6 months
Georgia		X				6 months
Hawaii				2 years	X	6 months
Idaho		X			X	6 weeks
Illinois		X		2 years	X	90 days
Indiana			X		X	60 days
Iowa	X				X	1 year
Kansas			X		X	60 days
Kentucky	X			60 days	X	180 days
Louisiana		X		6 months	X	6 months
Maine		X			X	6 months
Maryland		X		1 year	X	1 year
Massachusetts		X			X	None
Michigan	X				X	6 months
Minnesota	X				X	180 days
Mississippi		X				6 months
Missouri		X		1-2 years	X	90 days

	No Fault Sole Ground	No Fault Added to Traditional	Incompatibility Formula	Living Separate and Apart	Judicial Separation	Durational Requirements
Montana	X		X	180 days	X	90 days
Nebraska	X				X	1 year
Nevada			X	1 year	X	6 weeks
New Hampshire		X		2 years		1 year
New Jersey		X		18 months		1 year
New Mexico		X	X		X	6 months
New York		X		1 year	X	1 year
North Carolina		X		1 year	X	6 months
North Dakota		X			X	6 months
Ohio		X	X	1 year		6 months
Oklahoma			X		X	6 months
Oregon	X				X	6 months
Pennsylvania		X		2 years		6 months
Rhode Island		X		3 years	X	1 year
South Carolina		X		1 year	X	3 months (both residents)
South Dakota		X			X	None
Tennessee		X		2 years	X	6 months
Texas		X		3 years		6 months
Utah		X		3 years	X	90 days
Vermont		X		6 months		6 months
Virginia		X		1 year	X	6 months
Washington	X					1 year
West Virginia		X		1 year	X	1 year
Wisconsin	X				X	6 months
Wyoming		X	X		X	60 days

APPENDIX B

PROPERTY DIVISION

	Community Property	Only Marital Divided	Statutory List of Factors	Non-monetary Contributions	Economic Misconduct	Contribution to Education
Alabama		X		X		X
Alaska	X		X	X	X	
Arizona	X				X	X
Arkansas		X	X	X		
California	X		X	X	X	X
Colorado		X	X	X	X	
Connecticut			X	X	X	X
Delaware		X	X	X	X	X
D.C.		X	X	X	X	
Florida		X	X	X	X	X
Georgia		X				
Hawaii		X	X	X	X	
Idaho	X		X			
Illinois		X	X	X	X	
Indiana		X	X	X	X	X
Iowa			X	X	X	X
Kansas			X		X	
Kentucky		X	X	X	X	X
Louisiana	X					
Maine		X	X	X	X	
Maryland		X	X	X	X	
Massachusetts			X	X	X	X
Michigan		X		X	X	X
Minnesota		X	X	X	X	
Mississippi		X	X	X	X	X
Missouri		X	X	X	X	X
Montana			X	X	X	
Nebraska		X		X		

	Community Property	Only Marital Divided	Statutory List of Factors	Non-monetary Contributions	Economic Misconduct	Contribution to Education
Nevada	X	X		X	X	X
New Hampshire		X		X	X	X
New Jersey	X	X		X	X	X
New Mexico	X					
New York		X	X	X	X	X
North Carolina		X	X	X	X	X
North Dakota				X	X	X
Ohio		X	X	X	X	X
Oklahoma		X		X	X	
Oregon				X	X	X
Pennsylvania		X	X	X	X	X
Rhode Island		X	X	X	X	X
South Carolina		X	X	X	X	X
South Dakota				X	X	
Tennessee		X	X	X	X	X
Texas	X				X	
Utah						
Vermont			X	X	X	X
Virginia		X	X	X	X	X
Washington	X		X			
West Virginia		X	X	X	X	X
Wisconsin	X	X	X	X	X	X
Wyoming		X	X	X		

APPENDIX C

SPOUSAL SUPPORT FACTORS

	Statutory List	Marital Fault not Considered	Standard of Living	Status as Custodial Parent
Alabama			X	
Alaska	X	X	X	X
Arizona	X	X	X	X
Arkansas		X		
California	X	X	X	
Colorado	X	X	X	X
Connecticut	X		X	X
Delaware	X	X	X	X
D.C.	X	X	X	
Florida	X		X	
Georgia	X		X	
Hawaii	X	X	X	X
Idaho	X			
Illinois	X	X	X	X
Indiana	X	X		
Iowa	X	X	X	X
Kansas		X		
Kentucky	X	X	X	
Louisiana	X			X
Maine	X	X		
Maryland	X		X	
Massachusetts	X		X	
Michigan			X	
Minnesota	X	X	X	X
Mississippi				
Missouri	X		X	X
Montana	X	X	X	X
Nebraska	X	X	X	X

	Statutory List	Marital Fault not Considered	Standard of Living	Status as Custodial Parent
Nevada		X	X	X
New Hampshire	X		X	X
New Jersey	X	X	X	X
New Mexico	X	X	X	
New York	X		X	X
North Carolina	X		X	
North Dakota				
Ohio	X	X	X	X
Oklahoma		X		X
Oregon	X	X	X	X
Pennsylvania	X		X	
Rhode Island	X		X	X
South Carolina	X		X	X
South Dakota			X	
Tennessee	X		X	X
Texas	X		X	X
Utah	X		X	X
Vermont	X	X	X	X
Virginia	X		X	
Washington	X	X	X	
West Virginia	X			
Wisconsin	X	X	X	X
Wyoming				

APPENDIX D

CHILD SUPPORT GUIDELINES

	Income Share	Percent of Income	Extraordinary Medical Deduction	Child-Care Deduction	College Support	Shared Parenting Time Offset
Alabama	X	X	X	X	X	
Alaska		X	X	X	X	X
Arizona	X		X	X		
Arkansas		X	X	X		
California	X		X	X		X
Colorado	X		X	X		X
Connecticut	X		X		X	
Delaware			X	X		X
D.C.		X	X	X	X	X
Florida	X		X	X		
Georgia		X	X			
Hawaii	X	X	X	X	X	X
Idaho	X		X	X		X
Illinois		X			X	
Indiana	X		X	X	X	X
Iowa		X			X	X
Kansas	X			X		X
Kentucky	X		X	X		
Louisiana	X		X	X		
Maine	X		X	X		
Maryland	X		X	X		X
Massachusetts		X	X		X	
Michigan	X		X	X	X	X
Minnesota		X		X		X
Mississippi		X	X			
Missouri	X		X	X	X	X
Montana			X	X		
Nebraska	X		X	X		X

	Income Share	Percent of Income	Extraordinary Medical Deduction	Child-Care Deduction	College Support	Shared Parenting Time Offset
Nevada		X	X			X
New Hampshire		X	X		X	
New Jersey	X		X	X	X	X
New Mexico	X		X	X		X
New York	X		X	X	X	
North Carolina	X		X	X		X
North Dakota		X				
Ohio	X		X	X		X
Oklahoma	X		X	X		X
Oregon	X		X	X	X	X
Pennsylvania	X		X	X		
Rhode Island	X		X	X		
South Carolina	X		X	X	X	
South Dakota	X		X			
Tennessee		X	X		X	X
Texas		X	X			
Utah	X		X	X		X
Vermont	X		X	X		X
Virginia	X		X	X		X
Washington	X		X	X	X	
West Virginia	X		X	X		X
Wisconsin		X	X			
Wyoming	X					X

APPENDIX E

CUSTODY CRITERIA

	Statutory Guide- lines	Children's Wishes	Joint Custody Laws	Coop- erative Parent	Domestic Violence	Health	Lawyer or GAL for Child
Alabama	X	X	X		X		
Alaska	X	X	X		X		X
Arizona	X	X	X	X	X	X	X
Arkansas					X		
California	X	X		X	X	X	X
Colorado	X	X	X	X	X	X	X
Connecticut		X	X				X
Delaware	X	X	X		X	X	X
D.C.	X	X	X	X	X	X	X
Florida	X	X	X	X	X	X	X
Georgia	X	X	X		X		X
Hawaii	X	X	X		X		X
Idaho	X	X	X		X	X	
Illinois	X	X	X	X	X	X	X
Indiana	X	X	X	X	X	X	X
Iowa	X	X	X	X	X	X	X
Kansas	X	X	X	X	X	X	
Kentucky	X	X	X	X	X	X	X
Louisiana	X	X	X		X		
Maine	X	X	X		X		X
Maryland		X	X	X	X	X	X
Massachusetts			X		X		X
Michigan	X	X	X	X	X	X	X
Minnesota	X	X	X		X	X	X
Mississippi	X		X			X	X
Missouri	X	X	X	X	X	X	X
Montana	X	X	X		X		X
Nebraska	X	X	X		X	X	X
Nevada	X	X	X	X	X		X

	Statutory Guidelines	Children's Wishes	Joint Custody Laws	Cooperative Parent	Domestic Violence	Health	Lawyer or GAL for Child
New Hampshire	X	X	X		X		X
New Jersey	X	X	X	X	X	X	X
New Mexico	X	X	X	X	X	X	X
New York		X			X		X
North Carolina		X	X		X	X	
North Dakota	X	X	X	X	X	X	
Ohio	X	X	X		X	X	X
Oklahoma	X	X	X	X	X		X
Oregon	X	X	X	X	X		X
Pennsylvania	X	X	X	X	X	X	X
Rhode Island		X	X	X	X	X	X
South Carolina		X	X	X	X	X	X
South Dakota		X	X	X	X		
Tennessee	X	X	X	X	X		X
Texas	X	X	X	X	X	X	X
Utah	X	X	X	X			X
Vermont	X		X		X		X
Virginia	X	X	X	X	X	X	X
Washington	X	X			X	X	X
West Virginia	X	X	X		X		
Wisconsin	X	X	X	X	X	X	X
Wyoming	X	X	X	X	X	X	

Tips: Avoiding Financial Pitfalls

1. **Negotiate a reasonable settlement.** Get some professional advice from a CDFA™ or CFP™ to make sure you'll be able to live with the financial terms of the settlement – now and into the future.

2. **Don't live beyond your income.** Reduce your expenses – or increase your income – so that you are always saving something for a rainy day. Ask your financial advisor for help creating a budget if necessary.

3. **Think twice about keeping the family home.** Ask your financial advisor whether you can truly afford it, and ask them to show you what cash you'd have available for investment if you moved to a smaller home.

4. **Realize that you won't get everything you want in the property division.** Don't spend months and thousands of dollars fighting over furniture, appliances, or other personal items. Make a short list of "Must-Haves" and be prepared to compromise on everything else. Look at the big picture; is this asset best for your situation?

5. **Protect your Retirement Assets.** Make sure you have the QDRO filed as soon as possible.

6. **Use debt sparingly.** Get a copy of your credit report and close all joint accounts and all credit you do not use. Avoid maintaining balances on credit cards.

7. **Protect your credit rating.** Here are some tips:
   • get a copy of your credit report
   • close all accounts that you do not use
   • if you don't already have one, apply for a credit card in your name only
   • close all joint accounts and credit cards.

Tips: Going to Court

By the Honorable Kathleen M. McCarthy

1. Be clear as to your objectives. Present your issues in court with a proposed resolution. Use your own creativity instead of leaving that solely to the judge. Bring in all documents that support the facts and your theory.

2. Be civil and professional. Lawyers and litigants should address their remarks to the court – not to each other – and confine these remarks to the issues at hand. Engaging in personal attacks on opposing counsel and litigants is unprofessional and discouraged.

3. Respect everybody's time. Punctuality is important, and courtesy is important, too. If you're going to be late, advise opposing counsel and the court.

4. Dress appropriately. Your attire and person should be neat, clean, and professional – as though you're going for a job interview. This isn't a Saturday night date or an afternoon at the gym. You are in a court room, and your appearance should demonstrate respect.

5. Know the Rules of Procedure. Local or general court rules are the oil that keeps the engine running. Procedural *faux pas* get in the way of efficient administration of justice.

As a former partner in her own firm and a successful trial attorney specializing in the area of family law before being elected to the bench, Judge McCarthy is well respected for her knowledge and commitment to helping litigants and their legal counsel resolve highly complex legal and personal issues.

To-Do List

Item	Deadline	Completed
1 Initial meeting with my lawyer	10/23/06	✔
2		
3		
4		
5		
6		
7		
8		
9		
10		
11		
12		
13		
14		
15		
16		
17		
18		
19		
20		

Note: assign a completion date for every item you list here. These deadlines will help keep you focussed, and they'll let you know where you're on-track and where you're falling behind.

Notes

About the Authors

Fadi Baradihi is the president and CEO of the Institute for Divorce Financial Analysts™, the premier national organization dedicated to the certification, education and promotion of the use of financial professionals in the divorce arena. He has held the CEO position since 1998, and has been a financial consultant since 1991. Mr. Baradihi is a Certified Financial Planner™, Chartered Financial Consultant, Chartered Life Underwriter, Certified Divorce Financial Analyst™, and holds a Master of Business Administration.

Mr. Baradihi is a nationally known expert in this field. He has been interviewed and/or published by Lawyers Weekly USA, *Money Magazine, Bloomberg Wealth Manager, The Detroit News, The LA Times, Chicago Tribune, Kiplinger's Personal Finance, Journal of Financial Planning,* and *Divorce Magazine,* just to name a few.

Nancy Kurn is the Director of Educational Services and Legal Counsel for the Institute for Divorce Financial Analysts™. She is a Certified Public Accountant, Certified Divorce Financial Analyst™, and holds Master of Laws, Juris Doctor, and Master of Business Administration degrees. She is an attorney in MI and FL and is licensed as a CPA in MI. Ms. Kurn has published several articles on divorce-related financial issues in *Divorce Magazine.*

Ms. Kurn received her Juris Doctor from Thomas M. Cooley Law School in Lansing, MI, her Master of Laws in Taxation from University of Miami in Coral Gables, FL, and her MBA from Northwood University in Midland, MI. On the Dean's List in Law School, Ms. Kurn also received two American Jurisprudence Book Awards for the highest grade in Taxation of Partnerships and Business Organizations.

Diana Shepherd is an award-winning editor, published author, and a nationally-recognized expert on divorce, remarriage, and stepfamily issues. She has been interviewed by *The LA Times, The New York Times, The Chicago Tribune, The Globe & Mail, The Toronto Star, The National Post, Financial Post Review, The London Guardian, Harper's Magazine, Forbes Magazine,* and *Maclean's Magazine,* to name a few, and has been a guest on dozens of national television shows, including *"NBC Nightly News" "CBC Newsworld" "Canada a.m." "Money Matters"* and *"Report on Business".*

As well as being the former Editorial Director and co-founder of *Divorce Magazine,* Ms. Shepherd has had personal experience with divorce both as a child and as an adult. She has written or edited hundreds of articles about divorce-related issues since 1995 – including an online advice column entitled "Ask Diana" – and is the stepmother of three teenagers. She holds an Honors English Specialist degree from the University of Toronto and is a graduate of The Banff Publishing Workshop (The Banff Centre for the Arts).